He Blew Her a Kiss

INSPIRATIONAL STORIES OF COMMUNICATION FROM LOVED ONES WHO HAVE PASSED

Angie Pechak Printup & Kelley Stewart Dollar

Outskirts Press, Inc.
Denver, Colorado

Acknowledgements

First and foremost we would like to thank Tom and Judy for their amazing story, which was the inspiration behind this *He Blew Her a Kiss* series and inspired others to open up and share their experiences. A heartfelt thank you goes out to their children, Jay and Emily, who have been extremely supportive in this endeavor.

Our sincere gratitude to all of the wonderful friends both old and new who have submitted stories to us. A huge thank-you to Outskirts Press for all their wisdom and guidance in our first project.

Angie would like to personally thank her good friends, Nancy and Bob Partee, Jannina Hurdle, A.J., and Judi Armstrong, for their unwavering support; also, her wonderful life-coach friends, Daryl Frazier and Suzanne Marie Bandick. We would like to acknowledge Jill Dubbeldee Kuhn for the beautiful artwork on both the Web site and book cover; Cyndi Silva for the creation of the Web site, www.heblewherakiss.com, and for her friendship; and Mary McCammon, our photographer who has been a great friend and blessing throughout this journey.

And last but not least we would like to thank and express our deepest love to our families and close friends who have supported us and encouraged us every step of the way.

Dedication

We would like to dedicate this book to the memory of Tom and Judy McKelroy whose love affair of forty-two years touched the hearts of so many. We dedicate this to their loving family as well.

A Special Dedication

"Friends are the angels who lift us to our feet when our wings have trouble remembering how to fly."

It is with great joy and excitement that I am able to share this amazing, life-changing experience with my best friend of 35 years, Kelley Stewart Dollar. When I first began this unexpected journey in November of 2008, I had no idea that she would be a part of it. She has always had the ability to put pen to paper with an amazing end result, whether it be stories, poems, or letters.

One day I asked her if she would edit a few of the stories. Without hesitation she agreed. Her creative writing ability reached far beyond my expectations. I quickly realized partnering up with her was the perfect balance for this project.

As she has edited these true life stories over the past year, using her God-given talent, I have observed a joy and passion emerge that had long been buried inside of her. She is truly "on purpose" here walking with me on this path. I am honored to share this experience with her and so grateful for our life-long friendship.

Kelley, thank you for joining me in this "labor of love." You have and always will be a blessing in my life.

Angie Pechak Printup

Contents

.

Introduction

This story begins in the early 1990s. I was very involved in riding motorcycles, and since the Harley-Davidson was my motorcycle of choice, naturally I joined the Harley Owners Group. I struck up many friendships with people who shared the same passion as myself and in the process established some lifelong bonds.

Because of my involvement, I had the privilege of meeting Tom and Judy McKelroy. There were several couples, and we spent countless hours on day trips, overnight adventures, and just fellowshipping with one another. I learned to appreciate everyone's unique personalities. Tom himself was quite the character. A serious, responsible businessman by day, he was a free-spirited, humorous, and fun-loving guy "after hours." I was captivated by the sincere love that he shared with his wife, Judy. They made such a wonderful couple. Tom had the unique ability to lift the spirits of all those he came in contact with. He was a jokester at heart and quickly became the life of the party. Judy was the perfect match for him. Soft and kind-hearted, she stood by him no matter what. Their love for one another was evident in all that they did.

Eventually Tom and Judy had to move away, but we continued to keep in touch through cards, phone calls, and an occasional motorcycle trip. After an extensive battle with cancer, Judy passed away in 2008. We all felt the loss and knew it would be difficult for Tom. Judy was the love of his life.

It had been quite a while since the "old gang" had gotten together, so we decided to have a reunion of sorts, and Tom was eager to join us. We gathered around, sharing with each other the events that had transpired in our lives. It was a pleasant evening that we spent reminiscing and gazing at pictures taken from our many experiences together. Before the evening came to a close, Tom announced that he wanted to share a story with us. We sat mesmerized by his words as his story unfolded. When it was all over, there was not a dry eye in the room. All of us were so touched by the beautiful event he had gone through.

After leaving, I could not stop thinking about Tom's story. As I went to sleep, Tom and Judy were forefront in my mind. At 2:00 a.m. I sat straight up out of a deep sleep, and everything was crystal clear to me. Tom and Judy's story had inspired me to help others during their grieving process. My thoughts were to create a book where others could share and read similar stories. It was something I wanted to do so that people could feel the peace and comfort that Tom's love story so eloquently embodied. I have always wanted to help others, and this was the perfect opportunity.

Upon advice I decided to start out with a Web site rather than a book. It was a chance to see if others would be receptive to a different way of coping with their loss. As I progressed with my ideas, doors seemed to open. It dawned on me that I would like to include my best friend of thirty-five years in my endeavor. Kelley has been a very creative writer since I met her, and I felt her talents could be utilized in editing the stories we would receive. Assisting me on this journey has allowed her to do something that she loves, and at the same time help others through the grieving process.

A great many people struggle with the loss of a loved one. It has been our goal to help people understand that even though their loved ones are not physically with them, their spirits are. Our loved ones continue to watch over us, and in many instances will communicate with those they leave behind. Research confirms ways in which our loved ones communicate, such as dreams, a familiar scent or favorite song, their physical appearance, and more. Their method of communication is most often one we would easily associate with them. These ways of communicating are commonly referred to as ADCs or after-death communication. After many years of research, Bill Guggenheim and Judy Guggenheim wrote a wonderful book entitled, *Hello from Heaven*. The book goes into great detail about ADCs and includes many wonderful, true stories from people who have experienced communication from a lost loved one.

The stories we have compiled are also true to the best of our knowledge, with several of the contributors being close, personal friends. These stories represent some of the ways our deceased loved ones communicate, and sharing them has helped many in the healing process. The collection is what you might call a support group of stories. To date, this project has been embraced by many, and we so appreciate the love and support shown to us.

This is the first book in the *He Blew Her a Kiss* series. If you have a story, or stories, you would like to share, please go to our Web site at www.heblewherakiss.com and submit. Upon editing and approval from you, we will post your story either on the Web site, in our next book, or possibly both.

Much love and many blessings,
Angie Pechak Printup
Founder, *He Blew Her a Kiss*

He Blew Her a Kiss

The entire *He Blew Her a Kiss* concept can be credited to the following story, which will appear in every book of the series. We consider it to be our signature story.

He Blew Her a Kiss

High-school sweethearts living in a small town in Mississippi, Tom and Judy met in the seventh grade. He was so smitten that he asked her to sit with him at a movie after a 4H-club event. To his extreme disappointment she told him no. It was love at first sight for Tom, but his shyness prevented him from pursuing the love of his life again until the eleventh grade. It was then that he worked up the courage to ask Judy out again. This time she said yes, and from that point on they were committed to each other for life. They graduated from high school and while attending college, decided they couldn't wait any longer, so in 1967 they said their marriage vows and became husband and wife.

After the pair completed their college education, Tom

joined the air force, and they moved to Alaska. In 1972 he fulfilled his obligations to his country and left the service. Together, Tom and Judy moved to a city not far from their hometown. Tom began his career in the banking business, and Judy started teaching. Their small family grew to include two children, a boy and a girl.

After spending many years in the city, Tom had the opportunity to become the bank president back in the town he and Judy grew up in. Although they loved their city life and all the friendships they had cultivated, the kids had ventured out on their own, and the couple felt in their hearts this was the right move for them. So in 1999 Tom accepted the job. Judy had to stay in the city until they could sell their house. It was in this transitional period, during a routine mammogram, that Judy discovered a mass in her breast. It was indeed breast cancer, and in an effort to rid it from her body, she underwent a mastectomy in July 1999. After chemo, it was believed that she had gone into remission.

For eight years she faithfully went in for her yearly checkup, and happily, she was always cancer free. However, in the ninth year after her original battle with cancer had started, she began experiencing problems in her leg. Sadly, the cancer was back, and this time the invasive predator had moved into her bones, liver, and lungs. She underwent the insufferable sessions of chemo once again, but the disease had gotten too advanced for the treatments to help. On October 12, 2008, Judy's battle with cancer ended, and Tom lost his high-school sweetheart, love of his life, and best friend of forty-one years. Or so he thought . . .

Tom found himself alone in his house, experiencing a loss that he could never fully convey to anyone else. How can you possibly function when you become so separated from your soul mate?

Shortly after Judy's passing, Tom received a birthday gift from two of his relatives. It was a beautiful pail of candy, holding down a large, happy-birthday balloon with ribbons tied to it. He set the arrangement on the table with no realization that this would be the vessel for his communication with his beloved Judy.

A day or so later Tom returned home from work. Rain had settled on their town for the entire day, and it seemed as if nature itself were feeling just as melancholy as he was. Thinking about Judy, his glance fell on the arrangement sitting on the table. It was as if something had compelled him to look that way. Then it hit him. He was going to send his wife a message! Tom excitedly wrote his note on the ribbons, "To Judy, I love you soooooooooooooo much, love Tom." He then turned it over and addressed it, "This is for you, Judy, in Heaven."

Tom walked outside and looked around at the tall,

majestic trees in front of their house. He dropped his head, said a little prayer, then lovingly released the balloon in the air. He blew her a kiss and said, "Judy, here it comes." Tom watched it float ever higher in the gentle wind until it danced up to the clouds and disappeared from sight. Satisfied with his gesture of love, he went back in the house and settled down for the evening.

The next day Tom went through his familiar routine upon arriving at work. As he drove into the parking lot, he scanned around the building to make sure everything appeared as normal. Something caught his eye. He stopped the car and got out. Curious, Tom approached the walkway leading to the door of the bank. His breath stopped in his chest, and his heart began beating rapidly. There on the sidewalk was the balloon he had sent to Judy. Although it was deflated, it was otherwise in perfect condition. Lying next to it was the ribbon he had so lovingly written the note on. Comfort, love, and assurance washed over him because he knew beyond a shadow of a doubt that his prayer had been answered and Judy had received his message. It was Judy's way of telling him that everything was alright and that he didn't have to be sad any longer. She was still with him. He immediately told his coworkers and even called Judy's former coworkers to relate the story to them. Everyone cried tears of joy that day to celebrate Tom and Judy's undying love for one another.

Tom cherished his beloved balloon. He had it framed and proudly displayed in their home. It now served two purposes. First, it became a symbol to him of their love, and second, it afforded him the opportunity to share his story with others. Tom experienced how love transcends all when he sent his wife a love note, riding on the prayer and kiss that he blew to her.

A side note to readers:
Since the inception of this project Tom unexpectedly passed in May 2009. It has been a heartfelt loss to his family and friends alike. Perhaps God in his infinite mercy spared him further sorrow from a broken heart and reunited him with his beloved Judy. They would have celebrated their forty-second anniversary on June 6, 2009.

Inspirational Stories

Sometimes a single encounter is all that is needed to provide us the peace and comfort necessary to let go of those we have lost. The following section contains a variety of communications from single experiences.

Keeping the Family Tradition

Jay and Emily had always been part of a very close, tight-knit family. Their parents were wonderful people with a genuine love for each other and for their children. Even as the kids grew into adults they continued to do things together as a family. Since their parents, Tom and Judy, had such a deep-rooted love for the Mississippi State Bulldogs, it was no surprise that they purchased season tickets annually.

In October 2008 the family suffered their first devastating loss. Judy, who was the center of all their lives, succumbed to a longstanding battle with cancer. Their world turned upside down, especially for their father.

Tom did his best to cope and remain strong even

though the loss of his beloved Judy penetrated the very depths of his soul. He knew he had to move forward. His wife would never have wanted him to just give up.

With that in mind Tom returned to what felt comfortable to him. Tradition had become such a part of their family, and he believed it to be the best way to regain normalcy. Looking forward to the upcoming football season, he kept a watchful eye for any information about the team.

Unfortunately, Jay and Emily were forced to deal with yet another tragedy. In May 2009 they unexpectedly lost their father. Although Tom's passing was very difficult for them, they found comfort in the belief that he was now reunited with the love of his life. Their parents were together again, so they knew he was truly happy.

It wasn't until the fall of 2009 that Jay and Emily were faced with going to the football games without their parents, but they both felt it was important to continue the family tradition. It was their way of honoring such wonderful parents. Each of them had to deal with the emotions in their own way. A tangible sadness settled in as opening day approached. The absence of Tom and Judy was overwhelmingly apparent, but with undeterred resolve the children continued with their preparations.

Jay and Emily left early to enjoy the tailgating experience before the game. Upon arrival they realized they had forgotten the hamburger meat. Although that was to be the main course, they made do and had a wonderful time. The excitement built as the fans filed into the stadium. As kickoff commenced, so did the rain. It was a total downpour, but spirits were high, and everyone cheered their team on in spite of being soaked to the bone. The Bulldogs enjoyed a 45–7 victory and the celebration continued.

As Jay and Emily left the stadium and returned to the tailgating, they felt their parents were proud of them and their team for their victory. Almost as if on cue a perfect rainbow appeared over the campus. It was beautiful and couldn't have appeared at a better time. Jay and Emily believe to this day that it was a sign from God to confirm to them that Tom and Judy were together, happy and proudly watching out over their kids.

— *Submitted by Emily McKelroy*

The Dream

The sun cast a pink glow as it slowly climbed into the aqua blue sky. There didn't appear to be a cloud in sight as Wejay and her sister hurried out the front door. They could hardly contain the excitement that was threatening to burst inside them. At the end of the cove their mother, Helon, was waiting for them. She looked so pretty in her pink robe with beige, lace trim. They climbed into the car and off they went for a fun-filled day. They spent time shopping, visiting, and laughing about all sorts of things. Both girls cherished this time they shared with their mother.

The day went by all too fast, and they realized it was time to head back. The sun transformed into an orange ball of fire and began to disappear from the horizon as

Helon brought them home. She watched as her exhausted but happy daughters got out of the car and made their way into the house. They heard her say, "I'll see you soon," as they turned to wave good-bye.

The alarm clock sounded, and Wejay awakened to realize she had experienced the dream yet again. It was a welcome friend that always left her with a sense of contentment. After all, she had been having this same dream for forty years. It started after her mother passed when she was only twelve years old. As her thoughts drifted, her mind began to replay all the events of her childhood.

Wejay had an older sister and a younger brother. Her given name was Louise, but when her baby brother, Miles, attempted to call her, all he could say was "Wejay" and from that point on the nickname stuck. Her mother, Helon, was a happy-go-lucky woman who seemed to draw people to her. Always the life of the party, she was known to do crazy things. Her fun outlook on life endeared her to so many. Wejay's father worked as a traveling salesman for a radio station. The nature of his job required that he be away from home more than he cared to be, but it was necessary in order to provide for his family.

By the time Wejay turned twelve, her mother was battling ovarian cancer. It was extremely difficult for all of them. Her sister had already gotten married and had responsibilities of her own. It wasn't a difficult decision for her father to make when he allowed Wejay to stay at home with her mother. He thought it best for them to spend as much time as possible together, so he hired a tutor to help Wejay with her schoolwork.

Even though Helon was more or less confined to bed, she did have friends who visited her. Her sister, Wejay's aunt, bought a beautiful pink robe with beige lace on it. She wanted to be sure Helon had something nice to wear when she had company. Wejay remembered seeing her in that robe often. She enjoyed the time she had with her mother even though it was difficult seeing her deteriorate as she did. Sadly, Helon's battle with cancer ended much too soon. Her passing left them all devastated.

Just a few months after Helon passed, the dreams began. Over the years, whenever Wejay needs guidance from her mother or wants to be close to her, she has the dream. It is always the same at the beginning and end, but Helon has never failed to communicate with her daughter at those times when she needed her. Their bond has transcended the boundaries of life and death through dreams, showing us that love really can find a way.

— *Submitted by Louise "Wejay" Binkley*

Comfort from Clarise

Have you ever met someone whom you would never forget? Clarise was that kind of person. She could be characterized as a woman with a very open mind, a giving heart, a staunch supporter of what she believed in, and a very outspoken person. Her daughter, Angie, had many of the same qualities. When you put two people together who are very outspoken, inevitably an argument will erupt. Sometimes affection played a backseat in their relationship, but their love for one another was always a constant. Angie was the youngest of five children and the only daughter on top of that. Her mother always tried to instruct the best way she knew how. Even though it may not have seemed so at the time, she always had her daughter's best interest at heart.

There came a time after her parent's separation that just the two of them lived in Angie's childhood home. Her brothers had long since moved away, busy with their own lives. So many memories filled every room, and her mother's personality could be seen throughout the house. Eventually Angie moved out as well but always kept in contact with her mother.

Clarise took extremely good care of herself, always ate healthy, actively practiced yoga and overall was a very fit, attractive woman. It was because of her health consciousness that it came as such a shock to her family that she had been diagnosed with cancer. Despite all her efforts the cancer could not be subdued, and she lost the battle in May 1995. Angie was devastated and found it extremely hard to deal with losing a parent. Upon reflection she struggled with the fact that she had been unable to help her father more during that loss. Her parents may have been separated, but they were still very much a part of each other's lives.

After her mother's passing, Angie moved back into her home until other arrangements could be made. It was difficult, but amid her mother's belongings she felt a little closer to her. She longed to be able to talk to her mother again, if only to know that she was alright.

One night Angie climbed into bed, exhausted after her day. As she drifted off to sleep, her thoughts were of her mother and all the things she wished she had said while her mother was still alive. Then she heard the ringing of the phone. She picked it up only to hear her mother's familiar voice on the other end. "Hey, honey," she said. Angie had heard that greeting so many times before. Her mind raced. She knew she was dreaming, yet it seemed so real.

"Mom, where are you?" she questioned.

"Honey, I want you to know that I'm okay, and you're going to be just fine," replied Clarise.

All of a sudden the alarm clock went off, abruptly ending her heartfelt reunion. Angie knew she had been dreaming, but it had been so incredibly vivid, and she badly wanted to return to it to continue her conversation with her mother. Unable to do so, tears welled up in her eyes.

To this day she knows in her heart that her mother had contacted her to let her know she was okay. She did not have to worry about Clarise anymore. It was so comforting and she knew that her mother would continue to be with her in heart and in spirit.

— Submitted by Angie Pechak Printup

A Hug from Heaven

During Joe's time in the military he was provided an opportunity that he never really had growing up. There were twelve years between himself and his older sister, Maggie, and because of this age difference they never truly developed a close relationship. Maggie had moved out of the house while Joe was still a young boy. At one point she had even lived in Alaska. It wasn't until she moved to Yuma, Arizona that their relationship started taking off.

Stationed in San Diego, Joe was finally able to see and talk to his sister on a much more frequent basis. Eventually they ended up with only fifty miles between them. Maggie had moved to Los Angeles and Joe lived just north of there. As their bond continued to grow, Joe realized that Maggie was not just his older sister. She had become his best friend and closest confidant.

Over the years Joe enjoyed the many phone calls from his sister. Always eager to hear what was going on with Maggie, this particular call was one he would never forget. Joe found himself devastated as she revealed the terrible news. Maggie said that she had been diagnosed with breast cancer. He had tried to be strong for his sister, and it wasn't until he hung up the phone that the emotions raced through his body. Disbelief turned to anger, then to the frustration of loving someone so much and knowing there is absolutely nothing you can do to take such a burden away from them. Sadness overcame him, and all he could do was crumple to the floor, tears flowing.

Joe devoted himself to being there for Maggie. He may have been the baby brother, but he was determined to give his sister all the strength she needed. Maggie endured the insufferable treatments of chemo, and for two years the cancer hid itself in remission. Joe was thankful for whatever time he was blessed to have left with her. When the cancer did return, it was with a vengeance, firmly establishing itself throughout her body. Maggie lost the battle on January 10, 1988.

Although numbed by his loss, Joe clearly remembered sitting on a bench outside the hospital and noticing how beautiful the day was. The sky was blue and cloudless, the birds were singing, and it was a balmy seventy-five degrees around him. Strange, he thought, how can this day, a day of such loss and heartache, be such a beautiful day? Then he realized something. This was his first sign. Death is not ugly. It may be painful to those of us left behind, but death itself can be very beautiful. He felt his sister was nudging him to see that she was finally at peace.

Regardless of what he had felt that day, Joe's every waking moment was consumed with thoughts of Maggie. One day he found himself lying on the bed trying to take a nap. He screamed silently, "Please just let me know you're okay and you made it to the other side!" Joe sent his plea with every ounce of mental strength he could muster. Suddenly he felt himself being lifted off the bed by two figures. One gently cradled him and said, "Everything is fine, she made it. Don't worry about her, she is safe." Joe did not recognize the figures, but nonetheless the light and love that emanated from them gave him the warmest, most comforting feeling he had ever experienced in his life. It could have been nothing less than pure love. How appropriate that his sister had transitioned into the afterlife from a place called The City of Angels.

Twenty-one years later Joe can still recall those feelings from his "hug from Heaven" as if it were only moments ago. Maggie has come to him in dozens of dreams since then, smiling and laughing. How fortunate are those that can make contact with the other side. It is truly a blessing.

— Submitted by Joe Bach

A Love of Lilies

Young girls can be strongly influenced by the women in their lives. Such was the case for Jenna. Growing up, she spent a lot of time with her great-grandmother who was lovingly referred to as Nanny. She was a petite, soft-spoken, Italian woman whose loving presence grounded the entire family. When Nanny's husband died, the decision was made for her to move in with her daughter, Rose, Jenna's grandmother. Jenna loved going to see them. She would spend hours with Nanny watching television and reading books. Over time she learned to appreciate the same passion for flowers and music that her Nanny had, with lilies being their absolute favorite.

Jenna was thirteen when Nanny passed, and although it was a sad time for her, there were moments when she could feel Nanny's presence. It was always a comfort knowing she was there. It wasn't until Jenna began driving, however, that she started receiving her strongest signs. She attended Midnight Mass every year, and each time it was the same. Upon entering the church she would feel a slight gust of wind across her face and the overwhelming aroma of lilies. She knew beyond a shadow of a doubt it was Nanny letting her know she was with her. For several years this went on, but eventually stopped.

Jenna continued growing up and experiencing life's lessons along the way. One lesson proved to be very difficult, and she found herself becoming very depressed. In spite of the rough time she was going through, she managed to get herself up and go to her traditional Midnight Mass service. She was once again greeted with a gust of wind across her face and the overwhelming fragrance of lilies. Her heart welcomed the familiar presence that surrounded her. Nanny had come to comfort her and reassure her during such a trying time that everything would be okay. Jenna continued to smell lilies every day for an entire week.

It was also during this rough time that Nanny visited Jenna in her dreams. She didn't understand the dreams, but in each one Nanny would try to encourage Jenna to follow her. She would try, but was completely unable to move. When she awoke from the dream, there was always the strong scent of lilies in the room.

The dreams returned for several nights, always the same. The last dream, however, was a little different. This time Jenna was able to talk to Nanny. She questioned why Nanny wanted her to follow her. Nanny replied, "You'll find out one day." The answer startled Jenna, but before she could say anything else, she woke up.

The next day when Jenna returned home she was amazed at what she saw. There on the doorstep was a beautiful lily. Attached to it was a note with only one word, "Smile." Tears welled up in her eyes as she looked at it. She could hear the words Nanny said to her whenever she was upset, "Smile. It'll be okay."

Jenna has since moved forward, and her challenges have changed to celebrations. She thanks her Nanny for the strength and comfort that got her through her personal trials and tribulations.

— *Submitted by Jenna Printup Weaver*

Endless Love

*A*s Beau entered his apartment building, he saw her once again headed to the laundry. He made a quick dash to his apartment and hurriedly scooped up his dirty clothes piled in the corner. Here was his chance to see her again, and maybe this time he could find enough courage to strike up a conversation. But once again all he could do was admire from a distance. Oh, he had spoken once or twice and even talked to her about her poodle one day when she was out walking, but he couldn't seem to muster up the confidence to ask her out. Her name was Becky, and even though he hardly knew her, he was already quite fond of her. Fortunately for Beau, not only did they live in the same apartment building, they worked at the same place. Beau was an x-ray technician, and

Becky was a respiratory therapist.

After much prodding from a friend, Beau worked up the nerve to ask her out. It was the end of the work day, and Becky was getting ready to leave when the phone at her desk rang. On the other end was the mysterious admirer that her coworker had told her about, and it turned out that it was the same guy whom she'd seen at the apartments. She agreed, to his delight, and their destinies became intertwined.

Becky and Beau discovered that they were perfect for each other, and approximately two years after they started dating, they married. It turned out that they were unable to have children, so they devoted themselves to one another. They were happy and doing well in their careers. They moved several times and were always fortunate to make new friends wherever they went. Although Beau was a shy person, he was very likeable and adored by those who knew him.

Once they settled down, they decided to have a hot tub installed in the back yard. Becky suffered from back pain, and this helped to relieve it. She would come home every day and sink into its warmth and let it melt the pain away. Beau rarely joined her in the hot tub, but he would come and sit with her and together they would stare up at the heavens. He was knowledgeable about constellations, so he enjoyed pointing them out to her. They spent countless hours enjoying each other's company under the canopy of stars.

Things were going along smoothly until Beau had a recurrence of his seizures. When he was in his twenties, a drunk driver hit his car. His head hit the windshield with such force that according to the doctors, it caused his seizures. He had been controlling them through medication, which worked so well that the whole time he and Becky had been together the seizures only occurred a handful of times. This time, though, they were stronger, and one was severe enough that he had to take off from work for several days to rest. The doctor felt that the stress of long hours at work and double shifts had aggravated it.

After a few days off he went back to work. It didn't take long for him to realize this was not a wise decision. Beau knew he couldn't do his job properly as shaky as he was, so he got through the day as best he could. When he returned home, he got in the bathtub to unwind as he had done so many times before.

When Becky arrived home, she was met with silence. She knew Beau was home, so she called out to him. No answer. Assuming he was taking his usual afternoon bath, she went to the bathroom door. There was Beau, lying lifeless in the tub. He apparently had had one of his seizures and drowned while he was alone. Doctor's later confirmed it.

The days seemed unbearably long for Becky, the evenings even longer. She would talk to Beau even though she knew in her heart that he had gone on to a better place. Still, she found herself going to the gravesite every day in hope of regaining some sense of normalcy. Every evening she continued to sit in the hot tub, staring up at the stars, wishing Beau was there.

One evening the air seemed especially still when all of a sudden she felt a gentle breeze caress her cheek. At first Becky didn't really think that much about it, but after several occurrences it struck her as strangely familiar . . .

During the time Becky and Beau dated, his mother passed away from a massive heart attack. Being an only child, Beau struggled with his loss but maintained a strong front. Becky, on the other hand, had become very close to her mother-in-law and was devastated. After the funeral Becky and Beau were alone at her gravesite when out of nowhere Becky felt a gentle breeze touch her cheek and was overcome with instant peace.

Remembering that familiar "caress," Becky realized that Beau was also letting her know that everything was alright, and she would be just fine. The familiar calmness and peace that overcame her was indeed a welcome change to the endless emotional rollercoaster she had been on. Beau loved Becky with all his heart, and this was his way of saying, "I love you and will always be close."

Becky continued to occasionally feel these familiar "caresses" for a few months until she got stronger, and then they stopped. She truly felt her Beau was in Heaven and watching over her. Knowing this gave her the strength she needed to continue with her life.

— *Submitted by Becky Williams*

From Tragedy to Triumph

Marcel attended a local college but chose to live at home. Her best friend, Rachquel, went to the same college. They actually met in the tenth grade where there was an instant connection. It didn't take long to establish a special bond. They did everything together. If you saw one of them, you knew the other was close by. It had been like that since they had met.

One day Rachquel stopped by after class and asked Marcel to please run some errands with her. Of course, Marcel agreed as she always did, but she was a little puzzled at the vibes she was getting from her friend. It seemed as if Rachquel was almost pleading with her to go. Marcel jumped in the car, and they left.

First stop was Rachquel's grandmother. They visited

with her for a while. Then they went to Rachquel's mother's house. While they were there, they decided to eat. Normally Marcel would just make herself at home as instructed by her friend, but this time Rachquel fixed her a plate of food. Again, her behavior was odd. It felt as if she were waiting on Marcel, thankful that she was with her. They left and spent the rest of the day hanging out and reminiscing about the past.

It was getting late by the time Rachquel had to go to pick up her boyfriend, Jamie, from work. Normally Marcel would have accompanied her, but this time she had to excuse herself. She had a paper due for class the next day, so Rachquel dropped her off at the house.

An hour later Rachquel picked up Jamie from work, and he jumped in to drive. They were traveling through a neighborhood that quite honestly wasn't in the best part of town. The driver's side window was partially down because it was broken. Pulling up to a stop sign, they were startled to see a figure right next to the car. For a split second Rachquel saw a pistol shoved inside the window right against Jamie's head. She jumped as a blast exploded from the barrel. Frightened and panicked, she jumped out of the car and began to run. She could hear footsteps behind her getting closer and closer. Then as quickly as she heard the shots, she felt the burning sensation rip through her body.

Marcel had been diligently working on her paper, totally unaware of what her best friend was going through. Her god-brother was deep in conversation on the phone when it beeped. He answered the new call only to get the horrible news from a neighborhood friend that Rachquel and Jamie had both been shot. Marcel raced out of the house straight to the hospital.

When Marcel arrived, Rachquel was still clinging to life but the prognosis was not that good. She had been shot three times. Marcel clung to the belief that her friend was going to come out of this. She even saw herself taking care of Rachquel and being there for her. The thought of losing her friend just wasn't an option.

Jamie, being shot in the back of the head, was on life support. There wasn't really any hope for his recovery, and the next day he passed. Rachquel hung on for one more day before her body finally gave up. Marcel was devastated. Shocked and in denial, she just couldn't accept the fact that her best friend was gone. She wasn't prepared for that. How could this happen? Feeling lost and depressed she began to deteriorate. She started hanging around the wrong crowd, lost interest in school, and eventually dropped out. Missing Rachquel so much, she just didn't know what to do without her. As a last ditch effort she decided she would move and try to pick up the pieces of her life and put them back together.

One evening before she moved, she fell asleep. She began dreaming about Rachquel. They were together in a waiting room, preparing to have some professional pictures made. Marcel remembered thinking in the dream, "Oh, my gosh, I'm so glad you're alive. I guess I was just dreaming. I've missed you so much." Rachquel quietly got up and touched Marcel on the shoulder as she walked out of the room. She said, "I'll be back." Marcel sat there and waited until she realized her friend wasn't coming back. She woke up crying and upset but realized her friend was trying to communicate with her.

One night, after moving to another town, she settled down in her new bedroom to get some sleep. She lay on her side, facing the wall. She remembered closing her eyes and feeling the overwhelming presence of her best friend leaning over her shoulder. She then heard a voice call out, "Hey Boo!" That was the nickname Rachquel had given her. Her body froze. She was afraid to move and would not turn around. Through tears she told Rachquel how much she loved her and missed her. Rachquel responded by telling her the same and then said, "Don't worry. You're going to be okay." Marcel suddenly awoke in tears. She wanted to go back to that place where she could talk to her best friend but knew it was impossible.

She got up the next morning and for the first time felt that she really was going to be okay. She took what her friend said to heart and began the process of turning her life around. She enrolled in school, taking business courses, and ended up moving back home where she was accepted into nursing school. She succeeded in putting her life back in order and felt as if Smiley had played a major role in her recovery. Smiley was her affectionate nickname for Rachquel. As the name suggests, Rachquel smiled all of the time.

Marcel now knows that Rachquel is watching over her and smiling proudly. Eventually Marcel had a son who was born just one day after Rachquel's birthday. What a wonderful way to celebrate and honor her best friend.

— *Submitted by Marcel Williams*

The Doorway to Love

J ane had always been close to her father, and as she became an adult, their relationship deepened into much more of a spiritual connection. While not close in proximity, each living on opposite coasts of the country, they kept up with their relationship through phone calls and visits. Jane cherished her father's advice, so it was only natural that she would go to him with her concerns. Although having a very strong faith in God, she still found herself unable to move beyond her fear of death. She sought her father's wisdom regarding his belief in the afterlife. Her father told her that he did not doubt the afterlife at all and proceeded to send her several books on the subject, beginning with Dr. Raymond Moody's *Life After Life* in which he chronicles patients' very similar near-death experiences.

Over the years Jane and her father continued to encourage each other in their spiritual growth. As Jane grew in her own spiritual meditation techniques, she began keeping a journal. In this journal she recorded the lovely spiritual messages that came to her in her quiet times. Like everything else, she shared these messages with her father, and he was as supportive as always. In fact, he even joked with her about his hope that he could share with her how it was after he passed to the other side.

In 2006 her father's beloved wife and companion of forty years suffered two, near-fatal, health crises. It was November 5 of the same year when Jane received a call from her sister, informing her that their father had died in the night. She knew it had been a trying time for him, but the news was a complete shock. If anything, she had expected that call for his wife, Angelika. The following morning Jane and her sisters set out by plane from Boston to California. Feeling somewhat drained by everything that had transpired, she felt herself drifting off to sleep. It was at that time that she began to inwardly hear her father's voice. He was enthusiastically describing his feelings and experiences. Although she couldn't quite believe this was real, she faithfully transferred his words to her journal. She was overwhelmingly grateful to feel her father's presence again.

It soon became clear to Jane that all those years of spiritual bonding between them and learning how to listen with more than just outward senses had enabled her father to complete that one piece of the puzzle that tugged at his heart. She knew that he desperately wanted to prepare his wife for her own journey into the afterlife. He had always been there for her, and he had every intention of being there to guide her through this transition. Through the messages Jane recorded from her father, Angelika was able to find comfort and beautiful guidance, and within nine months they indeed were reunited.

Jane has written a book detailing the messages and lessons she received from her father. It is titled *WE ARE HERE: Love Never Dies.* The following is an excerpt that she would like to share with us.

"Angelika, honey, you'll be here soon. Don't worry about it. It'll be fine. I know that and now you won't be alone either. You're never alone! That's what I was really starting to feel before I left . . . it was all so peaceful. The shifting is really pretty easy. You just let go and they take care of the rest. I mean it. It's just the way I hoped it would be . . . only better."

"Angelika, do you feel my presence? I am here with you, always beside you, until we are in the same energy form—then you will understand so much and see so much that is unclear to you now. You know that I love you, that all is Love. All is permeated with the essence of God-self, which we call Love. You could say that the doorway you are entering is Love, and Love is the way. So, whenever you feel something that is joyful or pleasurable or that brings you peace, just breathe that in, and exhale what is not peace. It's a simple exercise. Notice the goodness—people's good intentions, a gentle touch, a kind word—breathe it in . . . and exhale what is not good and gentle and kind."

"And when you are alone, notice that I am with you. I will keep bringing you little signs of my presence. Breathe these in, along with the love I bring, along with the love of the unseen care-givers and angels who are here with you . . . Breathe in their subtle energies, and breathe out the sense that you are alone, that you are handling all of this alone. When I stand outside of my true self, I do not understand either, the timing of this, and why it is I cannot be there in person to help you. But that part of me, I know, is not real. It is not the part that is infused with enlightened love. For there are mysteries here—in this space of expanded consciousness—just as there are mysteries there. Here we breathe in, or expand to clear consciousness. We are one with divine intention."

"And so I hold this mystery in perfect peace. I love you perfectly as I am here beside you, and I wait with you in a state of sweet acceptance. Divine intention—over-will, you might call it, or the river of Love's wisdom—flows with a brilliance we cannot comprehend. We simply inhale the wonder of this mystery, and exhale all worry, doubt and fear. For it is known that you will be as I am soon. And as we sit together, let us practice acceptance, peace and joy. We, together, breathing-in what we cannot yet understand, and releasing our resistance to it—accepting the gifts it brings: For I am assured that they are many."

— *Submitted by Jane Smith Bernhardt*

If you would like to find out more information or purchase Jane's book, "WE ARE HERE: Love Never Dies," please visit her Web site at www.janebernhardt.com.

"Goodnight, Honey"

What could be more exciting for a child than growing up on a farm? Farm life is full of amazing, inspirational, and insightful things. There's never a dull moment. From sunup to sundown there is always something to do. Most of what Pat learned came from the time she spent with her grandmother, Rosa Pearl Jackson. To everyone who knew her, she was Honey.

Honey was the type of woman who was loved by all. She was faithful to her husband of sixty-four years, her family, and most importantly to God. Pat never knew a soul who had a bad thing to say about Honey. The only vice her grandmother was prone to was a little bit of gossiping that occurred on one of those old party-line phones. Overall she was a very amazing woman who loved everyone but had a special place in her heart for her granddaughter.

Pat did all kinds of things with Honey. They gathered eggs, picked flowers and vegetables, and while inside the house, she learned how to cook, can, and even crochet. Honey showed Pat how to cook her famous "chick and dumplins" a favorite of the family. In fact, she learned how to fix it so well that even her own mother was a tad bit jealous.

Living such a busy and physically strenuous life finally took its toll on Honey. She became ill and had to be hospitalized. The family spent as much time as they could with her, but the seizures became stronger and more frequent. It came to the point that she was unable to recognize who was with her or even control what she was doing. Pat said good-bye and kissed Honey on the cheek as they rolled her into ICU. There was little hope that Honey would recover.

The evening that Honey passed, Pat sat in her room filled with regret. The lyrics to a song came to mind, "I would trade all of my tomorrows for a single yesterday." She recalled a familiar scene. So many times she had seen Honey standing in the garden with her wide-brimmed, floppy hat to protect her from the sun, and the long-sleeved shirt she wore to protect her from the okra fuzz. Pat wished that she had called her grandmother more and gone to visit her more often. Most importantly she felt guilty about not taking the time to say "thank-you" enough for all that Honey did for her. She went to bed with childhood thoughts filling her head.

Then the most amazing thing happened. As she was trying to fall asleep, she heard Honey's voice as if she were right there next to her. In her soft, warm voice she said, "Goodnight, Pat." Pat quickly opened her eyes, hoping with all her heart she would see her grandmother standing there. The room seemed empty, but Honey's presence filled it. A feeling of recognition overwhelmed Pat. She truly believed Honey had been there to reassure her and to say goodnight one last time. She lovingly replied back, "Goodnight, Honey."

— Submitted by Dr. Patricia O'Kelley-Hughes

.

A Mother's Presence

The day started out as any other Saturday with the exception of a wedding Barbara was to attend. Her best friend's daughter was getting married, so of course, she would be there. She had just left the girls with her mother, Inez, and was headed to the church. Her daughter Jennifer and her niece Andrea loved being with their grandmother and spent every Saturday at her house. Inez was the magnet to which all in her family were drawn. She was the one who kept everyone well centered and grounded. Like any other grandmother she was patient and loving but had a stubborn streak in her that made her a fierce defender of those she loved. Unfortunately, it was that same stubborn streak that would change their lives forever.

Usually by the time the girls arrived, Inez would be up and about, cleaning what was already an immaculate house, but today was different. Earlier she had mentioned to her husband, Ted, that she was not feeling very well. As the morning progressed, it seemed to get worse. The girls had just arrived, and by now her tongue had started to swell. It was as if she were having an allergic reaction to something. Ted, their grandfather, called the doctor to see what they should do. When the doctor asked if she was having any trouble breathing, Inez said no. Her stubborn streak had taken over because she didn't believe it was that serious and it could be taken care of on Monday. As many people do, she assumed it was something that would soon pass. Knowing they would be unable to change her mind, everyone proceeded outdoors to sit on the patio while Inez stayed inside to rest.

A short time later they panicked as Inez came rushing out to them holding her throat. She collapsed, and they immediately called 911. With an ambulance on the way and feeling a little helpless, they called Andrea's mother, Deborah. She had been trained in CPR. Deborah was married to Barbara's brother, and they didn't live far away. She arrived quickly and performed CPR until the paramedics showed up.

In the meantime, Barbara had arrived at the church, and shortly afterward the ceremony began. Everything was beautiful. Flowers adorned the sanctuary and their sweet aroma filled the room. All eyes watched as the groomsmen and bridesmaids entered the room in exact cadence with the music. The organ chimed the familiar tune of "Here Comes the Bride," and with that cue the guests stood and turned to see the bride standing at the top of the stairs. She was radiant in her flowing white gown, and Barbara could not help but smile when she saw her.

It only took a moment for her to notice a small glow coming from behind the bride. She watched in wonder as it began to intensify. It then transformed into a brilliant white light that encased not only the bride but the large picture window behind her. Barbara suddenly felt an urgent tug at her elbow. She had been so mesmerized by the light that she hadn't noticed her son, Jonathan, enter the room. He didn't offer an explanation at first. He just told her they had to go.

Confused, Barbara hurried to the car. Once inside, Jonathan quickly filled her in on what had happened. Rushing to get back to her mother, they passed the church they were members of. All of a sudden Barbara felt a "swoosh" overcome her. She couldn't explain it, but later discovered that the precise moment she felt the "swoosh" was the exact moment the paramedics were able to briefly revive Inez. Ultimately they were unable to save her.

It was a difficult loss for the entire family, but Barbara believed in her heart that she felt the presence of her mother for that one fleeting moment. Later, she also found that the vision of the light at the church occurred at the same time that her mother collapsed.

Barbara continued to strongly sense her mother's presence for at least a month afterward. Sometimes it would overwhelm her so much that she would climb into the car alone, shutting out all distractions, and just sit and talk to her mother. Knowing that Inez was there listening to her, as she had done so many times before, brought Barbara immense comfort when she needed it the most.

— *Submitted by Barbara Bennett*

Brotherly Love

Typically, older boys don't want their baby sisters to hang around them. Not so in Helen's case. She and her older brother, Jay, were extremely close. With only three years separating them, it wasn't unusual for them to participate in the same things socially. Jay loved having his sister around, which worked out well for Helen. She was allowed to go on dates a little earlier than most her age because she would always double date with her brother. That made it okay in her parents' eyes. Jay and Helen spent a great deal of time together, so it was rather upsetting when their parents split up. Jay went to live with their father, and Helen stayed with their mother. Eventually Jay returned to live with his mother and Helen.

Time passed, and Jay became a man. It was time for

him to venture out on his own. He decided to move to another state where he met his first wife. The interactions between Jay and his family changed after that. Helen saw her brother less and less until it came to the point that she never got to see him. Conversations were few and far between, if any at all. Of course, all of this was hard to bear for Helen since she and Jay had been so close in their childhood. She knew her brother was going through some hard times himself, and it hurt deeply that she was being shut out. She wanted to be there for him, but it just wasn't meant to be.

As they grew older, the inevitable happened. Their mother became ill. Because of the severity of her illness, Helen tried to convince Jay to come see their mother before it was too late. Needless to say, Jay never came. Their mother passed, and he didn't show up, not even for the funeral. Helen tried not to hold any resentment toward her brother. She knew he was dealing with situations of his own and was just not capable of dealing with anything else at this point in his life. Although her loss felt doubled by the absence of her brother, Helen's life continued.

One day Helen was shocked to hear her brother on the other end of the phone. He had called to tell her about his wife's death. More importantly though, Jay was reaching out to his sister whom he had shut out for so many years. Helen loved her brother and was equally anxious to rediscover the bond that they had once shared.

Things were progressing quite well between them when Jay surprised her with the news that he had met a woman he was going to marry. His second wife readily accepted her new in-laws, and everyone got along just fine. Helen and Jay continued to stay in contact with one another and their bond grew. It was heartbreaking indeed when Jay shared the news one morning that he had a terminal illness. Helen didn't want him taken away from her so soon after their reunion.

Over the next month Jay's condition began to deteriorate rapidly. As it got closer to the end, his wife called Helen who immediately left town to be with her brother. She stayed and helped take care of him right up until the end. Although the ordeal was emotionally draining, she appreciated the fact that his wife allowed her to share what precious time he had left. After attending the funeral the following week, she returned home to her husband.

Helen hadn't been home for long. She and her husband, Ed, were sitting in the den, watching television and just relaxing. Her phone, plugged up and sitting on the kitchen counter, began to beep, letting her know she had a voicemail. "That's weird," she told her husband. "It never even rang." Helen went to her phone to check the message. "Hey little sister, this is your big brother. Just wanted you to know I'm doing fine. Call me when you get a chance."

Helen recognized the voice immediately. It was Jay! The only confusion she had was how strong his voice was. Her brother had been ill for quite a while, and his weakness was always reflected in his voice. This sounded like the old Jay, vibrant and full of life! It was then that she realized this message was from beyond the realm that we exist in. It was his way of letting his little sister know that finally all was well with him. She smiled to herself and thanked God for this wonderful gift. Helen could say her good-byes knowing that the bond between them would never be severed again.

— *Submitted by Helen Morris*

My Mother, My Angel

The importance of a mother's role in our lives cannot be emphasized enough. As children our whole world revolves around our mother. We seek her approval in all that we do. We share with her our successes and our failures. When she responds in encouraging ways, we gain confidence in ourselves. Being secure in the knowledge that her love transcends all other bonds affords us the peace of knowing we are never alone. When we are afraid or feel threatened it is our mother whom we turn to. Her fiercely protective nature provides us with a very strong sense of security. Our mother is by far the largest contributor to the foundation we need to transition from childhood to adulthood as happy, well-balanced individuals. Tragically some children lose that nurturing love at a much-too-early age.

Lauren was excited at the prospect of having the chance to sing on television. Her mother had come to pick her up so that she could inform the school that Lauren would not be there the following Monday. Bursting at the seams, Lauren jumped in the front seat of the car. Her best friend and best friend's brother got in the back. When all were safely in the car, her mother began to pull away from the school. Unable to control her excitement, Lauren climbed into the backseat to join her friends. Heading out, her mother made her way out of the neighborhood. She turned onto a major street, then swerved violently to avoid something in the road. Out of control, the car suddenly slammed to a stop.

It all happened so quickly. As Lauren regained her awareness, still shaken up, she saw her mother in what was left of the front seat. Evidently it had been a pole that had slammed the car to a stop. Sadly there wasn't even time to speak as she saw her mother take her last breath. Lauren cried out in frustration. She didn't even get to tell her mother that she loved her. Suddenly and without warning her life had changed forever, and the rest of the day became nothing but a blur from that point on.

Two years passed and Lauren, now twelve years old,

still struggled with the loss of her mother. There was a sense of unfinished business, a void that threatened to endlessly torment her. It is never in children's thoughts that their mother will not be there. It is taken for granted that Mom will always be around, but without the guidance, love, and support of her mother, Lauren felt in limbo. She argued endlessly with her father. It was not his fault. Fathers love their children but sometimes are not able to demonstrate that nurturing love that comes instinctively to a mother. As she crawled into bed, her frustration consumed her, and she longed to have her mother's love again.

Not sure if she was dreaming or if it was actually happening, Lauren sensed something. Opening her eyes, she saw her mother sitting at the foot of her bed. She was beautiful in a radiant, white gown, and although she seemed a bit thinner, Lauren could see that she was happy. Her mother never said a word, but her eyes said it all. She could feel the intense love and comfort in her mother's eyes. Lauren felt that she had come back to tell her daughter one last time that she loved her and that everything would be okay.

Even though Lauren was a young girl when it happened, she still remembers it as if it were yesterday. Her mother has become her "angel on her shoulder." Throughout her childhood and even now as an adult, whenever it is necessary, she draws upon the gift of comfort and love that her mother has so lovingly bestowed.

— *Submitted by Lauren Nichole Keele-Linbarger*

A Playful Presence

Geri listened to the silence that filled her house. For the previous four years her mother, Louise, had lived with her because of her failing health, but Geri never considered her mother a burden. In fact, they had always been very close, so she cherished the time they were able to spend together. She recalled toward the end, as it became harder for Louise to breathe, that she would tell Geri she was ready. Louise would say, "I'm in the short rows now," a phrase farmers commonly used as they harvested their crops. Since crops are most often planted diagonally, being in the short rows signaled you were close to the end of your harvesting work. Louise knew her time was limited and was trying the best she could to prepare Geri. Even though Geri knew her mother would have to leave, it never made it any easier. The silence of being alone again felt so heavy, and Geri longed for a sign that her mother was okay.

It was in the first month after Louise passed that Geri began having recurring dreams about her. The dreams would start in different places, but each would end the same way. Louise would get up out of the coffin she was laid to rest in and start walking around. Shocked, Geri would say, "Mother, I thought you were dead?" Louise would always look at her, laugh, and say, "I guess I'm not gone!" Geri couldn't help but chuckle to herself. Even in her dreams her mother still possessed that outgoing, direct, and somewhat humorous attitude that endeared her to so many.

The days went on for Geri as she attempted to get her life back into a normal routine. She had returned to work, so that filled up a good bit of her time. She and her sister spoke more frequently now, finding themselves immersed in stories and recollections of their mother.

Three weeks to the day Louise passed away and while Geri was dressing for work, the phone rang. Her sister was on the other end. Geri knew that sometimes their conversations could get lengthy, so she switched the phone to speaker and continued getting ready. She sat down on the bed, and as she bent over to put her shoes on, she noticed her cat, Domino, sitting on the floor at her feet.

As Geri began to tie her shoes, she felt something brush against her leg. Thinking it was her cat seeking some attention, she was startled to see Domino still in the same spot, busily smoothing the fur on her paws. Then she felt the bed move. She straightened up quickly to see an indention in the bed right next to her. It only took a brief moment for her to realize that it had to be her mother communicating with her. After all, she had prayed many times for a sign that her mother was okay. Although her mother's presence was initially somewhat of a surprise, it quickly turned to an incredible sense of peace. There were no words spoken, but the communication was very real. After that it became much easier for Geri to handle the loss of her mother, knowing that she was okay.

Right around this same time, Geri was getting ready for bed one night. It had been a long day. She climbed into bed and nestling her head into the pillow, she closed her eyes. Before she could drift off to sleep, she felt her pillow being pulled away from her. Geri got up and switched the light on. Her first thought was that her pillow had gotten stuck on something. She checked, and there didn't appear to be anything restraining it. Climbing back into bed, she once again felt a tugging as if someone were trying to pull the pillow out from under her. Suddenly she realized this must be her mother, only this time, a little more playful. The incident didn't frighten her. In fact, she called out to her mother this time and said, "Mother, if you're in the room, I miss you and I love you." Things seemed to calm down after that. It was as if Louise had been convinced that her signs had finally reassured her daughter that she was okay.

Another incident occurred at Thanksgiving. All the family had gathered at Geri's house. This was their first Thanksgiving without Louise and everyone missed her very much. Nonetheless, Geri sat with the rest of her family, enjoying their company and the conversation. Meanwhile, her five-year-old granddaughter, Christina, was fully engaged in her favorite game of sliding down the stairs on a blanket. Like most children do when they find something they enjoy, Christina would repeat it over and over. This time, however, she cut her game short, much to everyone's surprise. It wasn't until after the holiday weekend that Geri found out why.

The phone rang and it was Gina, Geri's daughter. She explained to her mother that her daughter, Christina, had questioned her about the door at the top of her grandmother's stairs. There was a bedroom upstairs but also a door on the left leading into the attic. Because the door wouldn't stay shut very well, Geri had attached a latch to keep it closed. Gina explained to her mother that during Christina's game of riding down the stairs, she had heard something at the door. Christina asked her mother if the doorknob could turn all by itself because it was turning back and forth without anyone doing it. That explained why Christina had so abruptly stopped playing. Geri realized with complete contentment that mom had been there for Thanksgiving after all.

— Submitted by Geri Maxwell

God's Light of Love

It takes special people to work with children facing terminal illnesses. It can be an emotional rollercoaster at times. Chloe is one of those special people. She is a nurse and works with kids suffering from brain tumors and seizures. Too many times she has been present when some of these precious children have gone home. She never realized how much her mother would help her in dealing with the losses she faced much too often.

Chloe's mother, Jean, was not one to get out much. She was content with being at home, doing her everyday routine. Things changed, however, when she found out she had cancer. Oddly enough, it seemed to bring her mother out into the world. She began volunteering at her church and doing things that were different from her routine. Perhaps she felt like others facing a terminal illness. The realization that your life might be cut short tends to motivate some people into living their life to the fullest with the time they have left. Whatever the reason, her mother became a different person.

Jean had to undergo chemo treatments which ultimately caused her to lose her hair. Chloe chuckled to herself when she thought of her mother's sense of humor over that. She would tell Chloe, "Well, when my hair comes back, I want it to be blonde and curly." It was her mother's attempt to downplay the harshness of the disease.

During her remission, Jean went to visit her other daughter, Lorry, who lived in Florida. She had originally planned to stay three weeks, but her cancer came back with a vengeance, forcing her to return home and be readmitted to the hospital.

Chloe lived approximately two hours from her mother and went to see her after her return. She couldn't explain the urgency, but she had a gut feeling that she needed to be there. As Chloe walked down the hallway approaching her mother's room, she saw a bright light spilling out of it. Rather than being startled, she was immediately overwhelmed by a peacefulness she had never felt before. It seemed as if Heaven itself had descended upon her mother. She continued into the room and the light dissipated. Her mother was lying in the bed, looking very peaceful.

Chloe and her mother spent a long time in conversation, sharing their regrets and cleansing their souls. She left that evening feeling that she and her mother had said their good-byes and they were both at peace with what was soon to take place.

That was twenty-five years ago, and the feeling of peace that came from the light was as real to her today as it was that day. That experience has helped Chloe when dealing with the loss of precious children. The light could have been nothing less than the love of God embracing his children. With that thought in mind and that sense of peace so real to her, she is confident that there is no place better we could be than in the arms of God, bathed in His light of love.

— Submitted by Chloe Knudson

Never Give Up

The excitement in the air was practically tangible. Renee had been accepted into the University of Memphis nursing program and her list of things to take care of before classes began that fall seemed endless. There was perhaps a touch of nervousness as well ... college ... nursing school. It was her first significant step toward adulthood. It only seemed natural for her friend to be there at her side.

The first stop was the scrub store where she was fitted for her very own scrubs. She purchased the necessary materials, and they headed for the university bookstore on campus. It was there that she picked up her stethoscope, blood-pressure cuff, pen light, scissors, and more. Her anticipation became overwhelming. She really was about to start nursing school! Reality crept in as she stood at the register, watching the total continue to grow. Wow, that was a lot of money. Renee began to question whether she was really ready for such a commitment. She knew nursing school would not be easy. Could she really do it?

As she attempted to push those feelings aside, she noticed the manager of the bookstore approaching her and her friend. He asked them if they would be interested in a two-week job. It would only be at the beginning of the semester when the bookstore was at its busiest. The girls looked at each other, shrugged their shoulders, and replied, "Why not?"

They followed the manager over to the lounge area so they could fill out the application. Renee placed her newly purchased supplies at her feet, pulled out a pen, and began to write. She was suddenly distracted as she felt a very light brush on her arm. She glanced over and realized there wasn't anyone there. She couldn't explain it, but immediately thought about her grandmother. All her worries and hesitations about school were gone. There was a definite sense of peace, and the anxiety that had begun to build inside her dissipated in the blink of an eye. She went back to the task at hand and completed the application.

Renee finally made it home after her very busy day, ready to show off all her new supplies to her mother and father. Of course, they were very proud of their daughter and the conversation revolved around her preparations for school. Later that evening as dinner was being prepared, her father looked at her and said, "You know, today is the anniversary of your grandmother's passing. It was eight years ago today." Renee felt the chill bumps as she recalled the brush on her arm earlier. She just knew it was her grandmother!

Growing up, Renee had been very close to her grandmother. She would spend the night with her all the time. They did a lot together including watching Shirley Temple movies and *The Wizard of Oz*. Another fond memory was her grandmother's Christmas tree. She remembered it being so bright and beautiful. Renee always felt special when she was with her grandmother so, of course, it was a difficult loss for a twelve-year-old girl to go through. But here she was eight years later about to start nursing school, and she felt in her heart that her grandmother would be very proud of her.

Renee's first semester proved difficult. She knew it was going to be hard, but not this hard. She had decided not to take the job at the bookstore but continued with a part-time job that she already had. She discovered that juggling work and studies just wasn't going to work for her. Her grades suffered, and she found herself with no other choice but to withdraw from school. Contemplating whether or not nursing was for her, she decided to take a semester off. In January, just three days before the new semester was to begin, she had a sudden urge to get back in school. She had been feeling very down and struggled with her decision to sit out a semester. She had to go back. She knew she could do this.

Two weeks into the spring semester, Renee quit her job and devoted herself to her studies. Her grades improved, and she began passing all her classes. She found herself at the end of her second semester of the program, never imagining she would actually make it this far.

Renee will never forget that simple brush on her arm. It was as if her grandmother were sitting right there saying, "Don't you give up, Renee. You can do it." She silently thanked her grandmother for believing in her and providing her with that little push of encouragement.

— *Submitted by Renee Canada*

A Promise Between Friends

Friends come and go in our lives and often we lose touch with them. Cheryl is of the firm belief that we meet people at the time that we need them in our lives. Sue Hunt was such a person. Cheryl first met Sue when she went to work for a local credit union. At first they did not get along so well, but it really didn't matter since they were in totally different departments. Their contact was minimal. After about six months, however, that changed. Now working together, they learned to tolerate one another.

Everything changed between them when they began playing softball on the company team. With the opportunity to really get to know each other, they became fast friends. Sue was a very devoted Catholic who took her lunch hour every day to attend Mass at a church close to where they worked. Cheryl herself had been raised in a Catholic home, but after the death of her brother, the family basically stopped attending. Even though Cheryl had drifted away from religion, she could still appreciate her new friend's devotion to God. Sue respected others and never forced her beliefs on anyone or judged anyone. But if you asked her, she was happy to discuss her relationship with God.

On many occasions Cheryl and Sue talked about God. As a result of some of their conversations they decided to take a trip. They traveled to Georgia, just the two of them, to a place where it was reported that Mary sometimes appeared. That trip became a defining moment in Cheryl's life. The night before leaving, they stayed with Sue's parents. They stayed up late, laughing together like a couple of schoolgirls and talking for hours. It was then that Cheryl proposed a pact. "Sue, if you die before me, let me know that everything we believe is true, and if I go first, I will somehow, some way, do the same for you." Sue agreed, and after the trip they would often joke about how they would do it.

Their friendship continued, but when Cheryl remarried after a painful divorce, her second husband was disliked by many of her friends. He insisted that she quit work and stay at home with their daughter. Because of her isolation, she eventually lost touch with many including Sue.

Cheryl ran into Sue a few times, but it was always in passing, and even though they promised to keep in touch, they never did. In spite of their time apart, Cheryl was devastated when she found out that Sue had passed away. It was even more painful when she discovered that her friend had suffered a long illness. It hurt her to know that she had not been there to provide support when Sue needed her most. She was also angry to some degree that her own self-absorbed life had caused her to lose touch with someone she considered to be "a wonderful light from God."

Cheryl attended the funeral the following day and was able to see the daughters and grandchildren that Sue loved so much. There was a sadness hanging over her for the loss of someone who had inspired her and given her so much love in her life. She regretted all the time she had wasted by not keeping in touch and not making more of an effort. It is so easy to take things for granted, never thinking twice that life is not guaranteed. It is up to us to make the most of the time that we have here. The only thing that gave Cheryl some sense of comfort was believing that if anyone would make it to Heaven, it would be Sue.

One evening Cheryl experienced a very odd dream. She was sitting in a bedroom that was hers but didn't look like hers. The phone next to the bed rang. Cheryl picked it up and said, "Hello?" In total amazement she realized it was Sue, and all she could say was, "Oh my gosh, how are you?" Sue replied that she was fine. Cheryl told her how glad she was to hear from her. About that time Cheryl's daughter, Reagan, entered the room. She excitedly told Reagan who was on the phone.

Reagan replied, "And?"

Cheryl exclaimed, "You don't understand. She is calling me from Heaven!"

Sue was laughing in the background as Cheryl turned her attention back to the phone and asked her, "Why are you calling?"

Sue replied, "We are allowed to call once a year and I wanted to see how you were."

Cheryl expressed her gratitude, then asked, "Shouldn't you be calling your daughters?"

Sue responded, "I will. I just wanted to see how you were and say hello."

Cheryl said her good-byes and hung up. At that moment she woke up and thought that it was really odd to have a dream about Sue because she hadn't thought about her in a long time.

It wasn't until the following day when Cheryl was on

her way to work that it hit her. Sue had actually held up her end of the pact they had made so many years ago. She had kept her promise and found a way to let Cheryl know that everything they had talked about and believed was true. God was there, and she should keep the faith. Sue had once again come through for her and inspired her as she had done so many times in the past.

Sometimes the people that we least expect can become some of our very closest friends. We may not know when or where we'll cross paths, but God blesses us with those we need in our lives at just the right time.

— *Submitted by Cheryl Cathey*

My Grandfathers and Me

Childhood memories often bring to mind warm, secure, happy thoughts of our loving grandparents. They influence our lives in a way our parents cannot. The famous author Alex Haley said, "Nobody can do for little children what grandparents do. Grandparents sort of sprinkle stardust over the lives of little children." Whether it was for a summer or for frequent regular visits, spending time with our grandparents allowed us a different look at life. As children we were able to see firsthand the values that our parents tried to teach us simply by spending quality time with the very ones that taught them.

Growing up, Julie was fortunate to have Grampa on her father's side of the family and Grandmother and Granddaddy on her mother's side. Grampa still worked, and he traveled frequently in his job as a printer, but whenever time allowed, he would show up unexpectedly at Julie's house. There were many times when they would come home to find him on the doorstep. Her mother would look at her and say, "You've been praying again, haven't you?" Julie's response was a simple smile and a nod of the head. Grampa spent as much time as he could with her, and she loved him dearly.

Julie would never forget the day her grampa passed away. It was a cold winter morning when she was awakened by people talking. It was not yet daylight, so they were speaking in hushed voices. She could tell by their tone something was wrong. It wasn't an easy thing for a six-year-old girl to understand. Overcome with sadness, all she could do was find an out-of-the-way corner to try and console herself as the adults went about the business of "making arrangements." Julie missed her grampa for many years after that, but found solace in the wonderful memories of him she kept in her heart.

Maybe it was because of the loss she had experienced, but now more than ever she wanted to be closer to and spend more time with her granddaddy in Mississippi. Her grandparents lived in a small town where everyone knew each other. A very relaxed and peaceful community, it was the complete opposite of the hustle and bustle of her city life just outside Chicago. Julie would spend at least two weeks on the farm every summer. It was a chance for her to go to see all her "cousins" and spend time with her granddaddy. She eagerly worked alongside him in the garden, picking vegetables although she seldom ate them! What she enjoyed the most were their long walks down a long, dusty road she knew as Granddaddy's Road.

Her granddaddy was a big man, and although he was tall and portly, he always had a walking stick with him on their journey. It became a ritual to stop at the small store in the center of their route to buy ice-cold bottles of pop. Her favorite was Nehi grape or root beer. Many happy memories were born from those lazy days of summer spent with her grandparents. Maybe there is truth to the quote that "grandparents sprinkle a little stardust on the lives of their grandchildren" because that was such a magical and joyful time in her life.

Julie continued to visit during the summers all throughout her teenage years, but times were not the same after Grampa died. The magic seemed to fade as Julie transitioned from a little girl into a young woman. Eventually she got married, and even though it was a happy occasion, it would have been wonderful if Grampa could have been there to see it.

One evening after Julie and her husband had gone to bed, she found herself face to face with her grampa again. He had come to her in a dream. Wanting to remember everything, she sat very still as she listened intently to him. He spoke as if he had never left her. He told her that she was going to be okay. He hugged her and then he was gone.

She awoke from the dream as the phone rang. Her husband reached over to answer the call. "It's your Mom." Instinctively Julie knew her granddaddy had died, and she told her husband that before she took the phone. She spoke briefly to her mother and after she hung up, she recounted the dream to her husband. Apparently her granddaddy had died at the exact same time that her grampa visited her in the dream. That was what he had meant when he told her that she would be okay. He had come to prepare her and impart to her the peace and understanding that she had felt with him as a child.

Julie and her husband attended the funeral and were amazed by the outpouring of love. People were there from all over the area. Most of them had been touched by his life in some way. The testament to how he lived was evident all around. One thing he had insisted on was no black, widow's garb. Only colorful dresses were to be worn by the women.

Although the sadness could be seen on all, from the young pall bearers and the grandsons to the white-haired men with tears, they were there to celebrate the life of a man who had done so much for others. While they paid their respects, Julie cried as she thought about no longer being able to see him sitting on the porch singing hymns or giving her a big bear hug when she visited. But then her grampa came to mind, and she knew that he and Granddaddy were keeping each other company and watching over her until she could see them again.

— *Submitted by Julie James*

My Guardian Angel

Windy knew her grandfather was not an average man. His unbreakable spirit could inspire anyone. While serving in the army he suffered a terrible accident that handicapped him from the waist down. Years later it even became necessary to amputate both his legs at the knees. In spite of his obvious physical limitations, he never let that get him down.

Windy was raised the majority of her life by her grandparents, so naturally their influence played a huge part in her life. She dearly loved her grandfather and deeply cherished the time they were able to spend together. When he passed away on April 3, 2004, a large void entered her life.

We're all familiar with the saying, "Time heals all

wounds." That wasn't the case for Windy. As each day passed, she found herself longing to be able to see him and talk to him. When she was younger, he would intentionally come up behind her and grab her on the neck. He knew it aggravated her, but it was always done in love. It was his way of showing her he cared. Oh, how she wished she could communicate with him just one more time!

Years passed, and Windy's life was hectic. Working mothers seldom have time to themselves, but even in the midst of all her organized chaos, Windy still thought of her grandfather every day, even at work. Filing charts had become almost second nature to her. She often found herself in her own little world while performing this task. One day as she reached down to insert a chart, she felt someone grab the back of her neck. She jumped up assuming that a coworker was playing around with her. As she turned, calling out the coworker's name, she realized she was all alone.

With complete conviction she knew it was her Papa, and he was right there with her. Windy was so thankful that her prayer had been answered. She felt her grandfather was with her all the time, watching over her, and he knew how much she needed him. With a simple, familiar touch her grandfather was able to convey his love and approval from the other side. Windy believes that he is looking down at her with pride in his heart for his beloved granddaughter. In his honor she chose to name her son Elgin, and she knows that he is so proud of her. His comfort and love came at just the right time, and she is forever thankful that he is always with her. He is her guardian angel.

— *Submitted by Windy Frazier*

I Will Always Love You

It was a Tuesday afternoon, February 16, 2010. After spending several weeks enduring a battery of tests and doctor visits trying to find out what was wrong, Wayne sat in the office of his oncologist. His wife Karen and his daughter Erica were right there by his side, mentally preparing for the news the doctor might have. They never expected to hear what the doctor shared next. Wayne was terminally ill, and the doctor gave him approximately six months to live. With heavy hearts they returned home.

Although it is a subject we are all reluctant to discuss, they knew it was necessary to go ahead and make some decisions about their future. Afterward, the rest of the evening was spent in casual conversation. Little did the family know that this would be the last conversation Wayne would have.

The next morning Wayne's health had deteriorated drastically. His comfort level continued to drop with each passing hour as well as his ability to respond verbally. They immediately phoned the oncologist and explained the increased intensity of Wayne's symptoms. The doctor recommended they get a hospice involved as soon as possible. The hospice nurse arrived, and after she had completed her evaluation, she announced that Wayne was an hours-to-days patient, meaning they had very little time left. The family spent the rest of that day and the evening trying to make sure he was as comfortable as possible. Trying to remain strong, they continued to reassure him and tell him how much they loved him. Although he was unresponsive, they were assured that he could hear everything. Karen and Erica knew in their hearts that it had to be frustrating for him. He was a very loving husband, father, and grandfather, and because of this debilitating condition, he was unable to respond to their affirmations of love. It was an emotionally draining day for all involved.

Early the next morning, Karen knew her husband was passing, so she begged him to wait just a little longer. She quickly roused Erica from her sleep. Everyone gathered in Wayne's room: Karen, Erica, her husband,

and their three children. The grandsons lovingly referred to their granddaddy as Poppabug. He was the
cornerstone of the family, and each one of them had
the opportunity to tell him how much they loved him.
With great respect they said their good-byes. Holding his
hand, Karen stood next to her husband and uttered her
final "I love you" as a tear trickled down her face. With
that, Wayne passed away peacefully, surrounded by the
people who loved him most.

The following evening they sat in the living room,
grieving in their own way. Erica sat on the couch with
the baby, and Karen sat on the floor, sobbing quietly for
the man she loved. In the background the television was
playing *Wheel of Fortune*, but no one was really paying attention. As Erica halfheartedly glanced at it, she
noticed the first puzzle was a song by Whitney Houston,
"I will always love you." Then what really caught her
eye was the contestant's name. It was Karen. This had
to be more than a coincidence. She rewound it, and
showed it to her mother. Karen looked at her daughter
a little shocked and said, "Do you think?" Erica thought
about it. Did she really believe it could be a message
from her father? She turned to her mother. "If Daddy
could give you a message, if God would allow him one
final message, what do you think it would be?" Tearfully
Karen replied, "Your daddy would say, 'I will always

love you, Karen.'" With understanding looks they knew that Wayne was leaving no room for doubt about his message of love to them.

— *Submitted by Karen Sands and Erica Lancaster*

A Decision-Making Dream

Growing up, Bobby was fortunate to have one of those fathers whom you could look up to. He was a man whose own integrity and morals were high, and he expected nothing less from his children. Being a fair man, he never jumped to conclusions and always gave his children the benefit of the doubt. That loyalty and trust, given without hesitation, molded Bobby into the man who would make his father proud.

Bobby was named after his father, Bob, who grew up in a small town in Colorado. Bob came from a family of devout Catholics and always carried at least one prayer book on him at all times. His faith instilled in him the belief that God was always with him and that guardian angels watched over him even in the darkest of times.

Fulfilling a commitment to his country, Bob served in the military during the Korean War. He was no stranger to death and being on the front lines, he witnessed first-hand the true tragedies of war. It was not hard for him to believe in guardian angels after being in the midst of so much killing and yet still survive.

People often struggle with issues after returning from a war, but Bob adjusted quite well. He settled into his civilian life and worked at a regular job for many years. One morning Bob sensed something wasn't right. He was only sixty but felt unusually bad when he woke up. Eventually he called 911 when the chest pressure did not relent. As the paramedics were taking him to the ambulance, his heart suddenly stopped. All his vital signs ceased, and the paramedics immediately began CPR. For seven or eight minutes they worked on him. Able to revive him, they rushed him on to the hospital. He was scheduled for tests the following day, and Bobby asked him if he was afraid or worried about them. His father replied, "No, I've been a lot closer to death than this before." Bobby didn't understand what he meant at the time but later came to the conclusion that his father was probably referring to his experiences in the Korean War.

Bob recovered from his close call and lived a fulfilling life. He spent as much time as he could involved in one of his biggest passions. An avid lover of polka dancing, he participated in many festivals. Most people look forward to the age when they can retire, but not Bob. After he passed retirement age, his son joked with him about why he hadn't stopped working. He slyly replied, "Heck, Son, I think they forgot how old I am. I'll just keep showing up till they tell me to go home." Bob worked because he wanted to, and he enjoyed staying busy. After seven years of living a happy and active life following the last health scare, he succumbed to a massive heart attack while attending a polka festival in Las Vegas. This time they were unable to bring him back. It was, of course, a devastating loss for the entire family.

As time moved on, Bobby had his own family and settled wonderfully into the role of husband and father. Everyone was happy and comfortable with the life they had created for themselves in Texas. However, Bobby had received a job offer in Colorado that was really hard to pass up. He struggled with whether to uproot his family and transplant them to an entirely different state. Sleep became more and more difficult as he tried to weigh the pros and cons of such a move.

One evening he was so restless, sleep seemed impossible. Eventually fatigue overcame him and he dosed off. That's when he started to dream. It was about his father growing up in Colorado, the very state he was contemplating moving to. Although it was before Bobby's time, he was able to picture and imagine things from the countless stories his father had shared with him about growing up with his brothers. Then he realized that in his dream his father was telling him that everything was okay and that Bobby's children would have plenty to do and would actually enjoy the relocation.

When Bobby woke up the next morning, he recalled the many times his father had come to him in dreams and realized this was different. His father was attempting to reassure him that this decision was not that hard to make and that everything would work out just fine if he accepted the new position. At that point Bobby became totally at peace about it all. His decision had been made while he slept. He thought about his father who believed in him when no one else did and how he always had his back. Thankful for his father's love and guidance, he uttered a simple yet sincere, "Thanks, Dad!"

We all have the ability to hear and see many things. It just becomes a matter of slowing down and paying attention to the world around us. The feeling that someone is watching over you, or someone is present, is not silly. Be receptive to it and you just might gain something from it.

— Submitted by Bobby Pechak

A Message from Beyond

Sometimes in life there are people that we forge an instant bond with. Their friendship feels like an extension of ourselves. Spending time together is comfortable; it's easy, and you know that you can share absolutely anything with them. Throughout our lifetime we may have many good friends, yet precious few will be our best friends.

Stephanie's best friend was a young man named Stevie. For about four years there wasn't a day that went by when they didn't talk or text one another. They did everything together: hanging out, riding around, and spending countless hours talking. They never judged one another. When one or the other had a problem or was just feeling down, they would ride around on the back roads with rock and roll music blaring as loud as it could. By the time the CD finished, their whole mood had changed. The stress would be gone, and at that point they could talk about it. Before you knew it, they would be laughing and having a good time just being themselves. There was no one else that Stephanie was closer to. She depended on Stevie for advice and moral support for every event or aspect of her life, and he looked to her for the same.

Although they cared about each other deeply, after about a year, circumstances changed. Stephanie found herself not agreeing with some of the things Stevie was doing. Distance began to grow between them, and they found themselves busy with their own lives. In spite of the fact they didn't hang out as much as they had before, they still kept in touch. One of the ways they communicated was by sending blank text messages. Words weren't necessary. It was just understood that it meant, "Hey, I was thinking about you and everything is good. I love you!"

Stevie still meant the world to Stephanie, so when he needed her, she was there with no hesitation. At one point he came to stay with her and her children. It turned out to be a godsend for Stephanie because for the next three months she was able to relive the times she and Stevie used to share. It was nice having him there, but it was only temporary.

A month after he moved out, Stephanie experienced

one of those weeks that you would like to erase from your life. It seemed as if one frustrating event after another occurred. She was working nights, and one evening after work her battery died. Thankfully she drove a 5-speed, so she was able to push it to get it cranked. On another occasion, on her way to the gas station, she ran out of gas. One morning she overslept and was late picking up her daughter. She was also aggravated with her roommate. It just felt as if everything was going wrong. If this trend continues, she thought, I'll lock myself up in the house and watch the Lifetime channel for the entire week. Finally, she looked forward to the next seven days. She would be off from work, and hopefully, things would improve.

Arriving home, Stephanie crashed on the couch. She was awakened by the phone ringing. It was her mother calling from the doctor's office. Stephanie's father might require surgery. After all that had happened recently, she begged her mother not to rush into any decisions. Before they could discuss it further, the doctor returned, so her mom said they would talk later. She hung up the phone and fell back asleep rather quickly. It seemed like only a moment had passed when her roommate woke her up again with phone in hand. Groggy from the interruption, Stephanie said hello. The instant she heard the tone in her mom's voice, the hair on the back of her neck stood straight up. Her mother began with, "Stephanie, I need you to wake up. Stevie was in an accident." Stephanie jumped to her feet. She heard herself cry out, "What?" Her mother proceeded to tell her that he had had a head-on collision with a truck as he rode his motorcycle. Hanging up, all Stephanie could do was sob uncontrollably. She had never lost someone that close to her.

Finally, after realizing her children were worried about their mother, Stephanie pulled herself together. Checking her phone for messages and missed calls, she noticed that several people had tried to tell her about Stevie. As she scrolled through, one message immediately caught her attention. It was an unopened text from Stevie. Her chest tightened, and she realized she was holding her breath as she opened it. It was just as she expected: a blank text.

Later, Stephanie visited the crash site. Just to be there took a big emotional toll on her. Once she arrived back home, she slept for twenty-four hours straight. When she finally got up, she found herself alone in the house, and she remembered her kids were at her mother's house. Tears came once again as she thought about Stevie. Suddenly her phone beeped. She picked it up to check, and once again there was a blank text message from Stevie's phone. Stephanie decided to call his number, and it went straight to voice mail. Curious, she began contacting some of his other friends and discovered that Stevie's phone had been broken for about two weeks. She wondered if he really was sending her a message to let her know he was okay. Her thoughts went back to a conversation they had once had. The discussion had been about death. They were both unsure of what happened after death, but they did talk about funerals and how they wanted their own to be. Stephanie remembered telling Stevie that she didn't know what she would do if something happened to him. Jokingly Stevie had replied, "Shoot, I'll just come back and haunt you!" He just laughed, and Stephanie knew he wouldn't really haunt her. She did, however, wonder if he was actually trying to communicate with her.

A week after Stevie passed away, Stephanie and her children went out to dinner. Her four-year-old daughter made the statement that she missed Stevie. With her emotions still raw, Stephanie was afraid she would break down again. As she fought back the tears, her phone beeped. It was the third and what would be the final text from Stevie. Calling the number back, she got the message that it was no longer in service. Looking up to the heavens, she had no doubt. The text messages they sent one another may have been blank but spoke volumes to them. By sending her the text when she really needed comfort, Stevie was letting her know in a way she would understand that he was fine and that everything would be okay. Stephanie has received numerous comforting signs from Stevie since then and knows without a doubt that he is watching over her and that she will see her beloved Stevie again one day.

— Submitted by Stephanie Boyett

Inspirational Stories

Some people have the wonderful opportunity to have more than one experience with loved ones who have passed. The next section contains multiple stories submitted by the same person.

Daddy's Little Girl

Against everyone's advice Willa walked onto the car lot in front of her. It was a small dealership, situated right next to a grocery store. She hoped that her luck would be better here at finding a car that was within her budget. She spotted a little Subaru sitting off to the side. Much to her excitement it was indeed something she could afford. She went inside and proceeded with the paperwork to make it her very own. Unfortunately, Willa could not take it home that day, so she left, filled with anticipation. It wasn't until a week later that she managed to get a ride back to the dealership. She followed the salesman to his desk to finalize the agreement and that's when she spotted it.

A chill raced down Willa's spine as she stared at the

license plate on the desk. She knew in her heart that this was more than a coincidence. The plate read "ART 0391." Memories flooded her mind in an instant. Willa and her father had been very close. His name was Arthur, but everyone called him Art for short. When she was younger, it was her father who drove her to all the horse shows. They spent hours on the road together, which further strengthened their bond. She was definitely Daddy's little girl, and it had broken her heart when she lost him a few years earlier. As a matter of fact her father had died in March 1991. When she saw the plate, "ART," after her father's name, and "0391," the month and year that he died, she knew she had come to the right place.

Willa couldn't get home fast enough. She proceeded to tell everyone about the tag and even went as far as taking a picture of it on her new car. She sent the picture to her family as proof. There was something unusual about the picture as well. You could clearly see a glow or aura around the car. In her heart she believed that her father had shown her beyond any doubt that he was still with her. To this day Willa drives with the assurance and comfort that her father is always with her, still looking after his little girl.

— Submitted by Willa Weller

The Phone Call

It seemed as if a lot had transpired the last few weeks. Willa had finally gotten a car along with a strangely unique tag to accompany it. She had also felt the excitement and happiness of knowing her father was still watching over her, even though he had passed a few years earlier. Each night she would fall into bed enjoying a good night's rest. This night would prove to be unique in its own rights.

Willa was in a deep sleep when the peaceful silence was broken. Her groggy mind tried to comprehend why the alarm clock was ringing when she came to the realization that it was the phone forcing her awake. Reaching over she picked it up and could hear the faint sound of a woman's voice. She sat up thinking that whoever was on the other end sounded as if they were very far away.

The woman said, "Willa, is that you?"

Willa responded, "Yeah, who's this?"

"It's your Aunt Bay. Are you okay?" Willa had never met this particular aunt, but she was aware of her.

"Yeah, I'm fine. Why?" said Willa.

"Well, I just wanted to check on you," said Aunt Bay. Then the phone went dead.

Quite confused Willa hung up and called her mother. She asked who Aunt Bay was. Her mother wanted to know why. Willa repeated the conversation she had had with her Aunt Bay. Her mother, somewhat surprised said, "That's impossible because Aunt Bay has been dead for years." She was an aunt on her mother's side of the family.

Although the phone call and the information from her mother caught her a little off-guard, she quickly recovered. Once again it was reassuring to know that she was being watched over by her loving father and her aunt. Even though she had never met Aunt Bay, it was clearly evident to her that family ties were never broken even after the passing from this life to the next.

— *Submitted by Willa Weller*

A Connection at Last

S tephanie slipped on her night clothes and climbed into her grandfather's bed. It had been a long day and it was finally time to go to sleep. Although tired, an uneasiness settled upon her, preventing her from falling asleep. You see, Stephanie's father had decided not to attend the funeral. Even though it was for his own father, there were extenuating circumstances, and he felt it best to avoid conflicts that would surely occur if he went.

It hurt Stephanie to see her father in this predicament. She was painfully aware of the situation between her father and grandfather. She adored her dad and she loved her grandfather but had never felt particularly close to him. Her father was very loving and outgoing while her grandfather was reserved and unapproachable. They seemed the exact opposite. She knew their relationship had not always been so strained.

Once upon a time they actually enjoyed doing things together. They shared a love of hunting, and many a day found father and son under the hood of a car or tinkering with a motorcycle. Everything changed, however, when her father divorced his first wife. Her grandfather did not approve. His disapproval became a permanent wedge between them especially after her parents married. In spite of the family history, Stephanie and her sister, Denise, would go to her grandfather's house every summer hoping to develop a bond with him. Even though they were his own grandchildren, he always remained somewhat distant.

Now, here they all were, gathered in her grandfather's house the night before his funeral. Typically this is the time that people find comfort in being together, leaning on one another for emotional support, and reminiscing about the past. However, this funeral had become anything but typical. Nothing seemed right.

Lying in bed, Stephanie was trying to close her eyes when she noticed a faint image appearing right before her. It grew, and to her amazement it became the outline of her grandfather standing there. He spoke directly to her saying, "Just tell him it's going to be okay." Stephanie knew right away he was referring to her father. She found herself feeling a comfort from her grandfather that was unfamiliar at best. It was as if her grandfather had transferred this sense of peace to her. He was trying to let his son know all was well, and he did not have to worry. Stephanie went to sleep that night, feeling for the first time that she had actually connected with her grandfather.

Early the next morning everyone except her father had gathered at the memorial service. The funeral was to be later that day, so after the service that morning, many returned to her grandfather's house. She saw her Uncle Sid who was her grandfather's brother, standing there. She approached him, and during the conversation it was discovered that Grandfather had appeared to Uncle Sid as well during the memorial service that morning. He gave him the same message for her father, "Just tell him it's going to be okay." They were both so excited about each other's experience that they rushed to tell her father.

Astonished at first, he contemplated what they had shared with him. He could see that it had profoundly affected them, so he agreed to go to the funeral. Just as Grandfather had said, everything went smoothly. None of the events he had anticipated occurred, and the service went well.

Stephanie's grandfather had finally done what he was unable to do while he was here. He had healed the rift between father and son. That simple communication from her grandfather had given her father just what he needed: closure. From that point on Stephanie knew everything was "going to be okay."

— *Submitted by Stephanie Shockley*

A Light of Love

Dean smiled as she handed the little bundle of joy up to her mother, Juanita. She gazed with love at her first granddaughter, Tina, and the bond was formed. Tina grew and soon had a little sister, Stephanie. Juanita, or MaMa, as she was lovingly called, adored all her grandchildren, but there was always an extra special place in her heart for Tina. Over the years their relationship strengthened, maybe in part because they were so much alike. There was nothing Tina wouldn't do for MaMa and vice versa. MaMa was very loving and outgoing, but crossing her was never a good idea. She still believed in strict discipline with her family.

Time passed and the grandchildren became adults, all busy with their own lives. Nevertheless, they continued to maintain a close relationship with MaMa. It wasn't until Tina was almost forty that her grandmother passed. She was such an outgoing and loveable character that it was quite a loss to everyone.

Not long after that, Tina put a nightlight in her room. She began talking to MaMa as she had done so many times before when suddenly her nightlight began to flicker. Every time she would talk to or think about MaMa, the light would flicker. Tina wasn't worried, for she knew in her heart that her beloved MaMa was communicating back. Whenever Tina, Stephanie, or their mother Dean walked into Tina's room, they would call out, "MaMa, are you here?" and the light would always flicker on and off, reassuring them of her presence.

Tina's light began this flickering shortly after Juanita's passing in 1994 and continues to this day. Amazingly, the bulb in that simple nightlight has never gone out, just as the bond they share has never wavered.

— *Submitted by Stephanie Shockley*

A Sweet Release

S ome families face incredibly tough decisions. Such was the case with Jannina. Born in Costa Rica, she was part of a very loving family. Her sister, A.J., was only two years older, and her brother, Ronnie, was seven when she was born. Because Ronnie suffered from an asthmatic condition, the humid climate of their homeland wreaked havoc on his health. Their mother, Amparo, had a difficult choice to make. She loved her children dearly but could not idly stand by and let her son deteriorate. It was with some degree of heartache that she and Ronnie left Costa Rica to move to the drier environment of Los Angeles. It was very sad for the girls to watch their mother leave, but they knew it was to help their brother. Amparo promised to come and get them when she was able, and she left them in the very capable care of their father and three aunts.

Seven years later their mother kept her promise. She and Ronnie returned to Costa Rica to bring Jannina and A.J. back to live in Los Angeles with them. Her father, however, did not go. Circumstances had led their parents to a divorce, and he chose to remain in Costa Rica.

Once in Los Angeles, Jannina's relationship with her brother began to blossom. They did a lot of things together, which included going to the beach, taking trips, and going out to dinner. They enjoyed each other's company and took every opportunity to strengthen their bond. As they got older, Ronnie met a wonderful girl named Donna, and the pair moved in together.

After living in Los Angeles for approximately twenty-five years, the girls were ready for a change of pace. Tired of the hustle and bustle of the city, Amparo and her daughters decided to move to Denver for a more relaxed atmosphere. Ronnie and Donna now had a daughter together and decided to stay put. Although they chose to live in different cities, distance did not prevent them from keeping in touch.

Three years after moving to Denver, Jannina found herself getting married. She and her husband decided to move to the South where some of his family lived. She continued to stay in touch with her family out West.

Nine years passed and everything was going fine until Ronnie was diagnosed with liver cancer. Jannina's mother and sister returned to Los Angeles in order to help Donna care for him. It didn't take long, however, for the cancer to ravage his body. With his health spiraling downward, Ronnie was admitted to the hospital. Jannina received the phone call she had dreaded. The doctors felt it would be best if she came out there because they didn't expect him to hold on much longer.

Immediately, she boarded a plane headed to Los Angeles. As she settled into her assigned seat and closed her eyes, she could feel the uneasiness building. How would she handle seeing her brother so ill? How could she truly convey the love she felt so deep inside for him?

As these thoughts rummaged through her mind, she suddenly had a vision. It was so real. She could see herself standing at the foot of Ronnie's hospital bed talking to him, telling him it was okay for him to go. The vision was so powerful! She snapped her eyes open and thought, "Where did that come from?" She closed her eyes again, and there was the vision. She told her brother, "Ronnie, it's okay to go. It's okay to go to the other side." Jannina opened her eyes and immediately turned to the passenger seated next to her. She asked him the time. It was 10:00 a.m. central time, which made it 8:00 a.m. on the West Coast.

She felt the tears welling up as she questioned herself. Why was she having these visions and why was she telling her brother that it was okay to go to the other side? She knew Ronnie had not been very spiritual. Perhaps out of her concern for him she was somehow trying to comfort him and help him to not be so afraid.

A flight attendant walking past noticed her tears. He asked if something was wrong, and she confided that her brother was dying. He took her to the rear of the plane to get some water and help her regain her composure in privacy. It was at that moment that she told the attendant she felt her brother had already passed.

As Jannina departed the ramp at the airport, she was greeted by Ronnie's best friend, Mundo. He took her hands in his, and as she looked into his eyes, she said, "He's gone, isn't he?" Mundo could do nothing but shake his head in agreement.

When she arrived at the hospital, rather than being upset and emotional, Jannina felt a sense of completeness. It was hard to explain, but she was not nearly as upset as she had thought she would be. She looked at her brother as he lay peacefully in the bed and gently took his hand. Very lovingly she uttered the words, "See you on the other side."

After speaking to her mother, things became much clearer to her. At the hospital Amparo had noticed that

Ronnie was anxiously watching the clock. It was as if he were expecting something. At 8:00 a.m. his mother assured him that Jannina would be there at any moment and to just wait on her. It was the exact same time that Jannina had the first vision on the plane. As she had the second vision, Ronnie took his last breath. She was overwhelmed with peace in the belief that she had indeed been able to see and speak to her brother before he passed. Her spirit was there to comfort him when he needed her most. It was her words that released him to that peaceful transition.

That night Jannina and her sister went to sleep in Ronnie's bed. She began dreaming and felt as if she were taking her last gasp of air, and then an incredible sense of peace and comfort came over her. The dream was so powerful it took her breath away as she awoke. She felt Ronnie had shared with her what he was feeling at his passing. She knew that the immense sense of peace, comfort, and love that had permeated her entire being was exactly what her brother had felt. That revelation gave her great joy.

After Ronnie's cremation they had a wonderful memorial service for him. Jannina had never felt such peace and comfort in knowing that her beloved brother was no longer suffering. She knew beyond a shadow of a doubt that his spirit was alive and well and in a wonderful place. She was able to let go of his physical presence with the absolute assurance that she would see him again.

— *Submitted by Jannina Hurdle*

Welcoming Party

Jannina's experience of losing her brother, Ronnie, to cancer made her incredibly stronger in dealing with death. She actually felt the immense peace and comfort that enveloped her brother in his passing, so she knew death was just a transition into something much, much, better. Just like any person who loses a loved one, she still struggled with the pain of her loss. It's only natural to be saddened by the absence of a loved one. Fortunately, she had been shown the beauty of such a transformation and found great peace in that.

Once again she faced an inevitable loss. Her father, Mario, had become very ill, and she was summoned to the hospital. He was not expected to live much longer. Her parents had divorced when she was a young girl, and her father had chosen to stay in Costa Rica where she had been born. Because of the great distance between them, she was regrettably unable to develop a close bond with him. He was, however, her father, so of course she wanted to be there to see him one last time. It was important to her to be able to say good-bye.

Jannina and her sister flew together to Costa Rica. When they arrived at the hospital, they found their father resting in his bed. During the visit Mario suddenly began to look beyond the girls. His attention was being drawn toward something unseen. The expression on his face turned from one of confusion to instant recognition. His eyes gleamed, and he began pointing just above and beyond their heads. He was smiling as Jannina looked at him and said, "Dad, is Ronnie there?" Mario turned his head in amazement and his eyes lit up. He emphatically shook his head to say yes and gazed at Jannina with a look of wonderment, as if she could actually see what he was seeing.

His gaze returned, and he immediately began pointing again as if singling out individuals. Jannina once again addressed her father. "Are they extending their hand to you?" With the same excited expression he shook his head to say yes.

With complete love in her heart Jannina told her father, "Go! They are here to help you to the other side. We love you, we forgive you, and we want you at peace." Mario rested and though he didn't depart at that time, he did pass away two days later on April 1, 2005.

There is always a sadness we go through when we lose a loved one. At the same time we can take comfort in knowing that no matter to what degree our loved ones may suffer here, they are going home to an existence free of pain. They are never alone. As Mario and so many others have expressed, loved ones who have passed before us are going to be right there waiting to welcome us home. We can look forward to a welcoming party like no other.

— *Submitted by Jannina Hurdle*

Rainbows of Joy

Paula's grandma was truly a special spirit. Her vibrant green eyes reflected the pure joy in her heart. The type of woman who never met a stranger, she had the unique ability to lift others' spirits. Grandma was quick to offer a kind word and would never allow a sad face around her. People could not help but be inspired, and her joyful attitude was infectious.

Paula recognized how fortunate she was to have such a positive influence in her life. Without question Grandma was dearly loved. When she passed, her loss was deeply felt by all whose lives she touched. Being the playful loving spirit that she was, Grandma was sure to have the last say. The day she passed, a glorious rainbow appeared in the sky. Paula knew it was her grandma because as soon as she saw it, she sensed her loving presence.

To this day when Paula sees a rainbow, she feels it is her grandma's reassurance that she is in a beautiful place, patiently awaiting the arrival of her loved ones.

— Submitted by Paula Timpson

Good-bye for Now

Saying good-bye to a loved one is never easy even if it's just a cross-country move, an extended trip, a vacation, or the end of a relationship. Whatever the reason, we never like to be separated. The loss can sometimes be very painful. The fear of separation can lead to depression and other medical problems. In the case of losing a loved one in death, the results can even be traumatic. What needs to be realized is that death is not the end, and it is not the last we will see of our loved ones. In fact, we should be happy for them because they are no longer confined to their earthly bodies, and their spirit is free at last.

Paula once again was faced with a loss. Her grandmother whom she dearly loved had passed, and now it was her Aunt Eleanor. She was her father's sister, a dear soul who had begun suffering from health issues including kidney failure. Having to undergo dialysis was challenging. Her body had become weary, and she was painfully aware of her physical limitations. Knowing her time was near, Eleanor had made peace with her family while at the same time trying to comfort them. Paula knew what was best and tried to keep a strong front, but she wasn't quite ready to say good-bye.

Leaving the hospital, Paula looked into her father's eyes. She could see the sadness there, but he too was trying to be strong. When they arrived home, Paula went to her room and began praying with the rosary. Attempting to cope with all the emotions swirling around inside her, she began writing. She decided to convey everything in a healing poem. That simple act enabled her to let her Aunt Eleanor go. As soon as she did, she suddenly felt her aunt's pure presence surrounding her.

Oftentimes Paula senses her aunt, usually when she's a little down. She knows Aunt Eleanor is keeping an eye on her and gently guiding her with her love.

— *Submitted by Paula Timpson*

Balloons

Sometimes the greatest lessons we can learn come from the afflictions of our most innocent of souls, our children. Each moment with them is indeed a blessing. Paula had the wonderful opportunity to know a young woman by the name of Dee-Ann. She had been diagnosed with hydrocephaly, an excess of fluid surrounding the brain, which cannot be absorbed into the body. There are treatments and procedures that can help, but in some cases there is little that can be done. Dee-Ann was one of those who remained with us much longer than doctors had expected.

Paula would oftentimes visit with Dee-Ann who was being cared for by her parents. She was in her twenties but still had the pureness of heart that a young child would have. In spite of her illness, she always had a smile on her face. The peace she exuded was a gift of strength to those around her.

Sitting by Dee-Ann's bed, Paula would create and read poetry to her, pray with her, and most of all, share her time with her. Her simple joy was a glowing testament to the protection God gives his precious children. Just as he does with adults, God never gives children more than they can bear. His strength is always there for each and every one of us if we only ask.

Many times we question why children have to go through debilitating illnesses and unforgiving diseases. All we can do is accept that there is a reason for everything. Though we may not know why, we can rest assured that when God calls our children home, they will be safe and secure in his love, and never again will a tear fall from their beautiful eyes.

There were many emotions present at Dee-Ann's memorial service. Although she had a relatively short life, she touched many people. Paula felt privileged to have known such a wonderful soul. Dee-Ann showed others that in spite of her condition, she could still have love, peace, and joy in life. Paula was thankful for the lessons she learned and the strength she gained.

At the end of the service there was a balloon release that seemed almost magical. The balloons danced upward into the sky as if carried by angels. They were small to-kens of love sent to Dee-Ann. To this day when Paula sees a balloon, she feels it is a reminder from her friend that her love is ever present.

— *Submitted by Paula Timpson*

Inspirational Stories

There are those people who are fortunate enough to have ongoing encounters. Judi Armstrong is one of them. Her experiences have proven to be an incredible gift from her son. She cherishes each and every one of them. His communication with her, whether in dramatic fashion or in very subtle ways, has continued to bring her peace and comfort after so many years. She found that sharing her stories has helped her immensely in the continuous process of healing and encourages others to do the same. The following section shows us that our loved ones really do watch over us.

Simple Gestures of Love

Raising young boys can be a challenge for any parents let alone a single mom, but that's where Judi found herself after the divorce. Mothers are there to be nurturing and compassionate, so it is sometimes more difficult for them to teach boys how to be men. As soon as you met Kevin and Sean, you could see the evidence of Judi's success. Both were well balanced and outgoing. It was often said that Kevin never met a stranger. He was kind to all and very popular throughout school. He was especially thoughtful to his mother. He made a point to show her how much he loved her by his actions. A simple gesture such as bringing her a yellow rose, not only on special occasions but often just because, never failed to bring a smile to her face. Her boys were the loves of her life, and the three of them shared a very strong bond.

One day Kevin, now twenty years old, gave his mother a letter that he had written. In it he told her that his life was getting ready to change for the better although he didn't know exactly how. It had been revealed to him in an incredibly vivid dream the night before. As Judi continued reading, she found words that she couldn't have been prepared for. Here was her twenty-year-old son, young, healthy, and vibrant, instructing her on how he would like his funeral to be carried out. He detailed his wishes about what he wanted to wear, including a particular ring. He wanted a family friend to play an instrument. He even specified songs he wanted played. Why would a twenty year old even be thinking about such things? As you can imagine, Judi was tremendously upset. Here was her own son talking as if he were about to die. She went directly to him and asked, "Why did you write this letter?" Kevin very calmly again explained his dream to his mother and tried to reassure her that his life would be changing for the better. Even though he did not know how it would change, he felt compelled to share the dream and his funeral wishes with his family in case something happened to him. This became a subject of conversation that Judi definitely was not comfortable with, so needless to say it was avoided.

About a week after Kevin had given his mother the

letter, he and his younger brother, Sean, had plans to attend a house party. One of their friends at the party was in the process of restoring a car, so naturally they wanted to go for a ride. Another friend, Randy, who was sixteen at the time, decided to drive. The car, not being completed, had running lights, but no headlights. As they headed down the road at a high rate of speed, they suddenly lost control and hit the bridge railing. The car flipped over on its top and careened to a stop. Randy and Sean had immediately been thrown from the car, but Kevin was still entangled in the mass of metal.

Judi awoke in the early morning hours to a ringing phone. On the other end someone informed her of the accident and told her that her youngest son, Sean, had been rushed to a nearby trauma hospital. At first she had no word of her oldest son or his condition. In a dazed state she rushed to the hospital to be with Sean. Several hours later, and after repeated attempts to find her other son, she received the devastating news that Kevin, her oldest, her baby, was gone. He had not survived the accident. Time stood still. She could feel what little strength and composure she had left just dissipate from her body. She fell to a crumpled ball on the floor, sobbing.

The first week after the accident Judi was distraught and helpless. Even though her soul ached from the separation, she still found it hard to believe he was gone.

She missed everything about him: his smell, his touch, and even the way he looked at her. Lying in her bed, she pleaded with God to give her a sign that Kevin was okay. Still, her inconsolable grief prevented her from stopping the tears, and once again she cried herself to sleep. This night, unlike the previous nights, would prove to be very different.

Judi experienced her own dream. In this dream her beloved son Kevin came down from Heaven to once again show his love for his mother. In his hand was an exquisite white feather, which he placed on her pillow next to her. He then returned to his ethereal home. As Judi was aroused from her sleep the next morning, she wondered about her dream. It seemed so real to her. She anxiously turned her head to check her pillow, and to her amazement there it was: a pure white feather, so beautiful that it could have come from the wings of an angel. She could hardly believe her eyes! She reached out to touch it. Amazed at what had transpired, Judi felt Kevin had revealed to her in his special way that he was okay. She unselfishly realized that through her loss, his life had indeed become much better. With that knowledge Judi felt an overwhelming sense of peace and calmness, which had eluded her thus far.

It has been many years since her son passed, and her collection of feathers from Kevin has grown. To this day she still has that original feather carefully and lovingly protected. Whenever Judi's heartaches become unbearable, Kevin continues to comfort her with simple gestures of love.

—*Submitted by Judi Armstrong*

The Comfort of a Caress

Approximately a week had passed since the horrible accident. Judi's youngest son, Sean, was still at the hospital in intensive care. Since she had been there nearly every waking moment, her mother came by to give her a break. Exhausted, Judi made her way home. The car seemed to drive itself. Once home she entered the bathroom to disrobe. As she stood in the shower, the stimulating droplets managed to penetrate the numbness that had shrouded her body, allowing the pain of what had happened to creep back in.

Afterward, Judi sat on the bed sobbing uncontrollably. Knowing how much she needed the rest, she stretched out on the bed and closed her eyes. Just as she started to drift off, she felt a distinct caress across her cheek, gently wiping the tears away. At the same time she caught the unmistakable scent of her son, Kevin. Judi felt right away that Kevin was there to give her a much-needed sign of assurance. Feeling the peace and calmness settle all through her body, she silently thanked him for his gentle compassion.

— *Submitted by Judi Armstrong*

Adornment of Feathers

J udi's youngest son, Sean, had grown up and married a wonderful girl named Michelle. Excitement abounded as they prepared to move into a new home. Having packed most of their belongings, Michelle went to the new house to do some last-minute cleaning in preparation to move in. She unlocked the door and went inside, anxious to get to work. With no curtains on the windows she noticed right away that something was going on in their new backyard. Peering out the glass, she looked closer. Shocked by what she saw, she immediately called her mother-in-law.

Judi listened as her daughter-in-law hurriedly expressed the need for her to come to the new house right away. Confused and a bit curious, she rushed out the door and headed straight to Michelle's. When she got to the house, she really began to worry. There was her daughter-in-law standing in the drive with tears in her eyes. When Michelle saw the worry on her face, she quickly assured Judi that everything was okay. She led Judi to the backyard, and they both stared in total amazement. The entire yard was adorned with beautiful white feathers. Together they collected some of them for keepsakes while the breeze carried the rest of them off. They looked at each other, realizing there could only be one explanation—Kevin. They both felt it was his way of blessing Michelle and Sean's new home. He had assured them it was the right choice by leaving his signature gift, an adornment of feathers.

— *Submitted by Judi Armstrong*

A Welcomed Visit

It had been a long day, and Judi's heart was heavy. She had been thinking about Kevin, as she often did. Judi knew that her son was with God and that all was well, and yet she still had days she struggled with his death. Usually it was during times like these that Kevin found a way to communicate.

One night after a restless evening, Judi finally went to bed. Not long after she fell asleep, she was awakened by the urgent barking of her dog. Worried when he wouldn't stop, she cautiously climbed out of bed to investigate. Much to her dismay the back door was wide open. Puzzled, Judi walked over and closed the door, checking the lock this time. She was almost positive she had locked it earlier. After she was satisfied that no one else was in the house, she walked back to her room. Familiarity struck her as she spotted a white feather lying on the floor by her bed. She knew right away that Kevin had given her the feather to ease her mind and remind her that he loved her.

So many times loved ones who have passed will utilize an object or a scent that is instantly associated with them. Over the years, Judi has had many communications with her son Kevin, beginning with the very first feather she received, which is detailed in her story, *Simple Gestures of Love*. Since then a white feather has been a calling card that Kevin has frequently used. Always benefiting from his sense of timing, Judi has gained great peace and comfort at just the right time.

— *Submitted by Judi Armstrong*

A House Guest from Heaven

For the entire weekend Judi felt unusually restless. Saturday would have been Kevin's thirty-ninth birthday, so naturally she found herself reminiscing about the past. Although thoughts of her son were pleasant, it seemed as if a cloud of anxiety had settled upon her. Whatever it was, she couldn't quite put her finger on it.

By Monday morning Judi had become almost agitated from the frustration of not being able to figure out her sense that something was going to happen. Sitting in front of the mirror, attempting to put on her makeup, she suddenly stopped what she was doing and called out to her son, "Okay, Kevin, are you trying to tell me something? If you are, please give me some kind of sign." Instantly the television switched on, and the blaring sound shattered the quietness that had filled the house. It was the television in the den, the one that she almost never used.

The noise startled her at first. She panicked for a moment, wondering if someone else was in the house. However, as soon as she confirmed that all the doors were closed and locked, she instantly knew it was Kevin. He had answered her in a unique way. It was clearly evident to her that she did, in fact, have a house guest even if it was ever so brief. This visitor was a welcome presence. She immediately felt the comfort that he always brought her, and the anxiety vanished. Judi smiled and went back to the task of getting ready. She left the house with the joy of a visit from her son filling her heart.

— *Submitted by Judi Armstrong*

A Joyride

It was a glorious day to be out enjoying the sunshine. Judi and her sister, Betty, were just driving around, listening to the radio and engaging in stories from their past. It was a day to let your hair down and relax, and that was just what they were doing. Amid their own laughter they heard a song suddenly blaring from the radio. It was, "People Gotta Be Free."

Betty immediately turned to Judi with a surprised look on her face. "Judi, that was one of yours and John's favorite songs."

"It sure was," Judi replied as she proceeded to turn the radio up.

John and Judi had been high-school sweethearts, and when they married they had two favorite songs,

"People Gotta Be Free" and "The Sun Ain't Gonna Shine No More." Betty looked at her sister and exclaimed, "Wouldn't it be funny if we hear 'The Sun Ain't Gonna Shine No More' next!"

Judi smiled and thought to herself, yeah that would be something.

As the first song came to an end, they looked at each other in astonishment. It was as if right on cue "The Sun Ain't Gonna Shine No More" began to play. Betty was amazed. What were the odds that those two songs would play back to back like that? Judi attributed it to Kevin right away, and Betty in complete agreement proceeded to roll down the window. She looked up into the sky and said to her nephew, "Thank you, Kevin. I love you."

— *Submitted by Judi Armstrong*

Scent from Above

Losing a child is a gut-wrenching tragedy no matter the circumstances. It is something you are never truly able to get over. True enough, you learn to adapt to it, and you learn to bear the heartbreak in your own way. But, sometimes it's just too overwhelming, and you find yourself unable to hold back the tears.

That is how Judi felt on this particular day. Her son Kevin had been on her heart and in her thoughts all day. As she sat there in her bedroom, tears streaming down her face, a familiar scent began to permeate the room. It became so strong that she would have sworn someone had sprayed it in abundance right there in her very room.

She recognized the scent immediately. Kevin had

always worn Lagerfeld, and she would often fuss at him about the amount he sprayed on. He smelled as if he had bathed in it. Worried that she might be imagining it all, she called out for her sister, Betty, who was in the other bedroom.

When Betty walked in the room, she immediately smelled the cologne too and asked, "Judi, do you have a man in here?" Then the recognition set in. "Oh, my gosh, Judi, that's the cologne Kevin wore!"

They both sat down on the bed, holding each other as tears of joy began falling down their cheeks. Judi said a silent prayer, thanking God for yet another sign from her beloved Kevin. God's timing was once again right on time.

— *Submitted by Judi Armstrong*

The Tiki-Hut Bird House

The entire week Judi found her thoughts drifting to her son Kevin much more often than usual. It had been nearly eighteen years since her tragic loss, and though her son was never far from her heart, he seemed especially close this week. Judi steered her thoughts to the task at hand as she pulled into Walgreen's parking lot. Her mission was to pick out a birthday gift for one of the ladies in her bowling league. She remembered seeing some decorative little birdhouses the last time she was there and thought her friend would love one.

Once in the store Judi found the display and began searching through all the birdhouses to find just the right one. She didn't intend to purchase it that day but instead would hide it in the back, behind all the other birdhouses.

The following day they were scheduled to bowl, so she would stop by and pick it up on the way.

The next morning Judi strolled into Walgreen's and headed straight back to the display she had thoroughly examined the night before. Carefully sliding all the birdhouses in front to the side, she proudly reached in to claim her hidden treasure. As she was retrieving it, the name Kevin practically jumped out at her. Right next to the birdhouse she had previously hidden the night before was an adorable little wooden house with the words, "Kevin's Tiki Hut," painted on the front.

"Wait a minute," she thought to herself, "I know this was not there last night." Judi had looked at each birdhouse the night before to make sure she picked the perfect one. In fact, none of the other houses were personalized at all! Where had this one come from? Without hesitation she snatched it up along with the gift and proceeded to check out.

When Judi arrived at the bowling alley, she gave her friend her birthday gift, but she was so ecstatic about Kevin's birdhouse that she had to show everyone. It was agreed by all that if Kevin had made a birdhouse, it would have looked exactly like the one she had bought. It seemed to reflect his personality perfectly. That is when it hit her. It was all so clear now. Today was Kevin's birthday! That is why she had felt him so close to her.

Judi stopped on her way home from bowling and bought a dozen yellow roses for her son, and a cupcake. She felt it befitting, considering that was exactly what he would have done for her. Once in the house, she set the roses on the table, pulled out the cupcake, lovingly placed a single birthday candle in the center, and sang a heartfelt "Happy Birthday" to her beloved son. Tears of joy trickled down her cheeks that afternoon because she knew Kevin was with her on his birthday. The birdhouse was so unique that she knew it had to be his way of communicating with her. Judi smiled to herself as she wrapped her heart in the blanket of her son's loving presence. All was well in her soul.

— Submitted by Judi Armstrong

A Tug from Above

J udi suffered the loss of her oldest son Kevin when he was only twenty years old. His death was a traumatic event for her, and it was difficult trying to recover from that. Being a very strong Christian, she prayed for a sign from God that her son was alright. In response to her prayers, Kevin appeared to her in a dream and gave her a wondrous sign, which could not be physically explained. Throughout the years after he passed, whenever Judi has been overcome with sadness and needed his presence, Kevin has given her some kind of sign to ease her heart.

This particular year, 2010, marked the twentieth year anniversary of Kevin's death. She missed him so much. February 28 would have been his fortieth birthday and because of that, her thoughts were on him more so than normally. It had been a really bad month for her. Nothing had gone right, and her spirits were low.

Judi was at home one morning when the phone rang. It was her sister, Betty. She asked Judi to go to the cemetery that day in honor of Kevin. Judi replied, "Betty, you know I never felt like Kevin was actually there. I don't know if I really want to go." Eventually her sister talked her into going.

Upon arriving, they drove to the section of the cemetery that contained their family plots. Judi had been there only a few times since she had laid her son to rest. Because of her faith she had not felt it necessary to go. His spirit had long since left his body. Besides, she felt he was always near and watching out for her.

They walked around with heads down as their eyes scanned the many headstones. Judi felt that she was in the right spot, but they just couldn't find the grave. Betty headed back toward the office to check for the exact location. As Judi turned and began walking away from the area, she felt a distinct tug on the back of her shirt. It was as if someone were trying to stop her. She halted dead in her tracks. Her first thought was Kevin. As she turned back around to where she had felt him, she stood alone. With a smile of understanding she immediately spotted his gravesite. She felt as if her heart had escaped from her body just for a second. It was long enough for Kevin to impress upon his mother a message: "Mom, wherever you are, I am right there with you."

Right then and there Judi decided she would be coming much more often to visit her son. She felt that in this place he had further confirmed what she knew in her heart.

— *Submitted by Judi Armstrong*

Share with us

If you have a story that you would like to share, please submit it to our Web site at www.heblewherakiss.com. We would love to hear your reactions to the stories in this book or on our Web site. Please let us know if you have a favorite story and if it touched you in any way by posting your comment on the guestbook at the bottom of the page.

If you prefer, you may also post a comment on our Face Book page at www.facebook.com/heblewherakiss. We hope these stories will provide you with the peace and comfort they have for us and for those who have submitted them.

About the Authors

*A*ngie Pechak Printup and Kelley Stewart Dollar, being lifelong friends of thirty-five years, have teamed up to compile stories intended to help others heal after losing a loved one. This idea originated from an amazing story that happened to a friend named Tom, after his wife and soul mate of forty-two years passed away from cancer in 2008. The first story in this book portrays their amazing love affair.

Angie has an extensive background in health and fitness, earning a master's degree at the University of Memphis in 1991. She has been teaching CPR and first aid for more than twenty years and was a volunteer EMT for five years.

Kelley has twenty-five years of experience in printing and graphic arts. She has always enjoyed creative writing and has written poetry for thirty years. Because of her ability to empathize with people, she is able to capture the essence of their emotions and experiences in each story.

Because they were best friends, it was only natural for them to work together, and combining their talents has allowed them to bring this wonderful book to you.

LaVergne, TN USA
15 September 2010
197150LV00009B/42/P

9 781432 760922